Your Soul's
Gentle Shepherd

Charles J. Callan, O.P.

Your Soul's Gentle Shepherd

Why You Can Have Absolute Trust in Jesus Christ

SOPHIA INSTITUTE PRESS®
Manchester, New Hampshire

Your Soul's Gentle Shepherd: Why You Can Have Absolute Trust in Jesus Christ was originally published by John Murphy Company, Baltimore, Maryland, in 1915 under the title *The Shepherd of My Soul*. This 1999 edition by Sophia Institute Press contains minor editorial revisions to and deletions from the original text.

The cover artwork is the mosaic *The Good Shepherd*, in the Mausoleum of Galla Placidia, Ravenna, Italy (photo courtesy of Scala/Art Resource, New York).

Sophia Institute Press®

Box 5284, Manchester, NH 03108

1-800-888-9344

www.sophiainstitute.com

Nihil obstat: M. A. Waldron, O.P.S.T.M., and J. A. McHugh, O.P.S.T.Lr.

Imprimi potest: J. R. Meagher, O.P.S.T.Lr.

Imprimatur: J. Cardinal Gibbons

Library of Congress Cataloging-in-Publication Data

Callan, Charles Jerome, 1877-1962.
    [Shepherd of my soul]
    Your soul's gentle shepherd : why you can have absolute
        trust in Jesus Christ / Charles J. Callan.
      p. cm.
    Originally published: Shepherd of my soul. Baltimore, Md. :
J. Murphy, 1915.
    Includes bibliographical references.
    ISBN 0-918477-93-X (pbk. : alk. paper)
    1. Bible. O.T. Psalms XXIII — Commentaries. 2. Bible. O.T.
Psalms XXIII — Meditations. I. Title.
BS1450 23rd.C3 1999
223'.206 — dc21   99-18651 CIP

99 00 01 02 03 10 9 8 7 6 5 4 3 2 1

Contents

The Lord is my Shepherd; I shall not want.

He maketh me to lie down in pastures of tender grass.

He restoreth my soul.

He leadeth me in the paths of justice for His Name's sake.

Yea, though I walk in the valley of the shadow of death,

I will fear no evil, for Thou art with me.

Thy rod and Thy staff, they comfort me.

Thou spreadest before me a table

in the presence of mine enemies.

Thou anointest my head with oil; my cup runneth over.

Surely goodness and mercy shall follow me

all the days of my life, and I shall dwell

in the house of the Lord unto length of days.

Editor's Note: Some of the biblical references in the following pages are based on the Douay-Rheims edition of the Old and New Testaments, and others are based on the Revised Standard Version. The latter are designated by the following symbol: (RSV). Where applicable, quotations from the Douay-Rheims edition have been cross-referenced with the numeration in the Revised Standard Version, using the following symbol: (RSV =).

Introduction

No images more beautiful could have been chosen under which to picture the character of our Lord and the souls He came to redeem than those of a shepherd and his flock. As nothing on earth could more fitly illustrate the infinite love and sacrifice of the Savior than the enduring labors and tenderness of a shepherd, so nothing here below could better portray the multiple wants of our spirits than the needful, dependent nature of sheep.

Beyond the knowledge we possess of our Redeemer, only a slight acquaintance with the characteristics of pastoral life, as it exists in oriental countries, is needed to discern the charming fitness of these comparisons. The similarity is at once striking and most easily understood.

Hence it is that our Lord, as well as those who described Him before He came, so often appealed to shepherd life when speaking of the Messiah's mission; hence, also, it is that He was so fond of calling Himself the Good Shepherd, and of alluding to the souls He loved as His sheep.[1]

It is the purpose of the pages that follow to trace some of these beautiful and touching resemblances between the shepherd with his flock, on the one hand, roaming over the hills and plains of Palestine, and, on the other hand, the Savior of the world with the souls of men, pursuing together the journey of life. We have taken as our guide, in noting these charming likenesses, the Twenty-second Psalm,[2] or the psalm of the good shepherd, every verse of which recalls some feature or features of pastoral life, and sings of the offices, tender and varied, which the shepherd discharges toward his flock.

As this shepherd psalm was composed and written in the Hebrew tongue, the language of ancient Palestine, we have employed here a literal translation from the original language, simply because it expresses much more

[1] John 10.
[2] RSV = Ps. 23.

beautifully and more exactly than does any rendering
from the Latin or Greek the various marks and characteristics of the shepherd's life and duties. The oriental lan-
guages, like the people who speak them, are exceedingly
figurative and poetic in their modes of expression; and
hence, for our present purpose, it is only by getting back
as closely as we can to the original that we are able adequately to appreciate the beauty and poetry of that simple
but charming life about which the psalmist is singing.

Although the shepherd psalm refers, in its literal
sense, to the human shepherd attending and providing
for his sheep, it has also another higher meaning, which
its author gave it, and this has reference to Christ in His
relations with the souls He has made and redeemed. It is
by reflecting on this sense of the psalm, and on all His
gracious dealings with us, that we are enabled to realize
how rightly and justly our Savior is called the Shepherd
of our souls, and how beautifully the psalmist, in the
shepherd psalm, has depicted His relations with us.

And how important this is! How much it means for
our spiritual welfare and spiritual advancement to reflect
on the many mercies of Christ and on the love He bears
for each one of us! If the considerations that follow help

you to appreciate more fully and love more ardently
the divine Shepherd of souls, who daily and constantly
throughout our lives is ministering to our spiritual needs
and trying to further our eternal interests, the desire
and aim which prompted their writing will be fully and
perfectly realized.

Your Soul's
Gentle Shepherd

Chapter One

Christ is
the Good Shepherd

It was announced by the prophets of old that the Messiah who was to come should bear the character of a good shepherd. He was to be a shepherd, and His followers, the faithful souls that should believe in Him and accept His teaching, were to be His sheep. It was foretold that He would select and purchase His flock; that He would choose them from out of the vast multitudes of their kind and gather them into His fold; that He would provide for them and guard them against every evil; that He would lead them out to green pastures and refresh them with the waters of rest.

"He shall feed his flock like a shepherd," sang the prophet Isaiah. "He shall gather together the lambs with

His arms, and shall take them up in His bosom, and He Himself shall carry them that are with young."[3] In like manner did Jeremiah, referring to the comforting advent of Christ, liken the offices which the Savior would perform toward His people to those of shepherds toward their flocks. "I will set up pastors over them," said the prophet, speaking in the name of Jehovah, "and they shall feed them; they shall fear no more, and they shall not be dismayed; and none shall be wanting of their number. . . . Behold the days come, saith the Lord, and I will raise up to David a just branch; and a king shall reign, and shall be wise, and shall execute judgment and justice in the earth."[4]

The prophet Ezekiel also prophetically portrayed the Savior's character when he pictured Him in the capacity of a shepherd visiting and feeding his sheep: "For thus saith the Lord God: Behold, I myself will seek my sheep, and I will visit them. As the shepherd visits his flock in the day when he shall be in the midst of his sheep that were scattered, so will I visit my sheep, and will deliver them

[3] Isa. 40:11.
[4] Jer. 23:4-5.

out of all the places where they have been scattered in the cloudy and dark day. And I will set up one shepherd over them, and he shall feed them, my servant David; he shall feed them, and he shall be their shepherd."[5]

And when at length the Savior did appear in the world, He declared, not only by His life and example, but in explicit terms, that He was the fulfillment of these prophecies — that He was, in truth, the Good Shepherd, and that His followers were the sheep of His fold. In the tenth chapter of the Gospel according to St. John we have His own words to this effect. There He tells us plainly that He has not come as a thief and a robber, to steal, to kill, and to destroy; that He is not a stranger, at the sound of whose voice the sheep are terrified and flee away; that He is not a hireling, who cares not for the sheep, and who, beholding the approach of the wolf and the enemy, flees and leaves the sheep to be snatched and scattered and torn.

The Savior is not any of these, nor like them. He is the Good Shepherd, who enters the sheepfold by the door, and not as the thief and robber who climb up some

---

[5] Ezek. 34:11-12, 23.

other way. To Him the porter opens, and He calls His sheep, and they know His voice and follow Him, and He leads them out to pasture, to rest, and to abundant life. And this is not all, for He protects and guards His sheep. By day and by night He is ever near them. When circling the green plains, or beside the still waters, or when asleep beneath the silent stars, the sheep are protected by their Shepherd. Faithfully He watches His dependent flock. And at the end, as a proof of His love and fidelity, He generously lays down His life for His sheep.

Chapter Two

Christ the Good Shepherd
is trustworthy

We cannot appreciate the beauty of this picture of our
Savior under the symbol of a shepherd, nor can we later
understand the detailed description which is given of Him
through the spiritual meaning of the shepherd psalm,
without first taking into account some of the features of
pastoral life as it prevails in eastern countries. For us of
the western world it is difficult, and at times next to impossible, to represent to ourselves the life and customs of
the Orient; and in particular do we find it hard to picture
in our minds and to understand the simple poetry of that
shepherd life for which Palestine has always been known.

Time has little changed the scene of the Savior's
earthly labors. The people, their manners and customs,

their life and occupations remain much the same now as when the land was graced by His sacred presence. Thus today, as in those olden times, all the level country east of the river Jordan, as well as the mountains of Palestine and Syria, serves as vast pasture lands for innumerable flocks and herds. The country throughout is essentially pastoral in its character, and the care and raising of sheep constitute the chief industry of the people. From sheep, the people are furnished with nearly all the necessities of life: meat, clothing, milk, butter, and cheese.

The shepherd exercises vigilant care

The care of sheep is a delicate and, in many ways, difficult task. It is not that they are froward or hard to manage, for of all animals, sheep are the most tender and gentle; nor again, that they need abundant nourishment in the way of food and drink, since they require water but once a day, and can maintain life and strength on a plain which, to the naked eye, seems little more than a barren waste of sand. But because, in other respects, they are exceedingly timid and helpless creatures, especially in times and places of danger, the burdens which their welfare and safety impose upon the shepherd,

while paternal and winning, are, nevertheless, arduous
and manifold.

There are the changes and hardships of the climate:
the cold and frost in winter, and the heat and drought
of summer; there are the long, rough walks, the steep
and dangerous passes which they must climb and descend; there are perils from robbers, wolves, and wild
beasts, which not infrequently demand the shepherd's
utmost watchfulness and care. The oriental climate is
such that they can graze nearly the whole year through.
And whether they are grazing on the wide, open plains,
or huddled snugly within the sheepfold, the shepherd
must provide for their varied needs.

His vigilance can never cease. He must lead them out
to pasture and to water; he must guide and protect them;
he must gather them into the fold at night or into caves
and enclosures, at times, during the day, to shield them
from great danger, whether from enemies or violent
weather; and upon all occasions, he must be prepared
to defend them, even at the risk of his own life.

The folds, or sheep pens, it must be observed, into
which the sheep are gathered for rest or protection
are not roofed over or walled in like a house. They are

enclosures left open to the sky, and consisting simply of a high wall of rough stone, to protect the sheep from the attacks of wild beasts and from prowling marauders who threaten their safety by night. It often happens that several flocks, belonging to different shepherds, will graze on the same pastures during the day, and will be penned in the same sheepfold at night. While the sheep are sleeping, and the shepherds nearby are taking their needed rest, the door of the fold is carefully locked, and another shepherd or porter is left on guard, lest perchance a hungry bear or wolf scale the wall and destroy some member or members of the sleeping herds.

Sheep trust in their shepherd

Early in the morning the shepherds come in turn and rap at the door, and to each the porter opens. Then each shepherd calls his flock by name; and they, knowing his voice, follow him, and he leads them out to their pastures. There is never any confusion, for each flock knows its own shepherd and obeys him alone. Other shepherds they will not heed, and from the voice of strangers they will flee.

It is a beautiful scene to see a shepherd with his flock. First, we must remember that he never drives them, but leads them; and they follow him with instinctive love and trust wherever he goes. He usually carries a rod and a staff. The staff he uses, when need be, to assist the sheep along dangerous paths and narrow passages; the rod, to protect and defend them if they are assailed by enemies or beasts of prey.

Another evidence of their implicit love of their shepherd and trust in his goodness, and also of their obedience to his voice and commands, is beautifully manifest when several flocks are led to drink at the same stream or well. Although the sheep need to drink but once a day, the shepherds never forget, throughout the day's roaming, that they must lead their flock to water. And as the drinking places in Palestine are comparatively few, it often happens that several herds, whether from the same or neighboring pastures, will arrive simultaneously at the same spring. But here again, there is neither trouble nor confusion. When they have drawn near to the place of water, each shepherd gives a sign to his flock, and, obedient to his voice, the respective flocks lie down and patiently await their turn to drink. The troughs are then filled with the refreshing water, and, when all is ready, a shepherd calls and his flock at once rises and comes forward to drink. The sheep being satisfied, the shepherd gives another sign, and they promptly return to their previous place of rest, or move quietly away to their pasture, as the shepherd may direct. Another flock is then called up, watered, and led away, and so on, in like manner, until all have been duly satisfied.

With this passing glance at shepherd life, we can better understand and better appreciate the likeness between the character of the Savior and that of the good shepherd. We can see how apt it was that our Redeemer should choose a shepherd, with his multiple and tender cares and duties, to illustrate his own watchfulness and loving kindness toward the many wants and needs of our souls.

For we are, indeed, His sheep. He has called us, we have heard and understood His voice, and He has gathered us into His flock and fold. He has literally vindicated for Himself in our regard all the attributes and qualities of the good shepherd, so far as described, and as still further depicted in every verse of the Twenty-second Psalm. This is called the psalm of the good shepherd, because, in it, the psalmist, under the symbol of a shepherd, prophetically foretold the character of the Messiah, our

Savior. The psalm has, therefore, a twofold meaning: in its literal sense, it deals with the faithful shepherd, ranging with his flock over mountains and plains, and providing for their every want; and in its spiritual and prophetic meaning, it relates to our Creator and Savior, caring for our spiritual necessities.

Let us see how this is. And so that we may better perceive the application in detail, let us take this shepherd psalm, part by part, and see how beautifully it describes the whole person of Christ as God, and in his capacity as Redeemer — in all His tender relations with us, and toward the various needs of our souls.

Chapter Three

Christ always cares
for your soul

∞

"The Lord is my Shepherd;
I shall not want."

How full of meaning and how comprehensive are these simple yet beautiful words which introduce the shepherd psalm! They at once sum up the whole round of the shepherd's life: his duties, his solicitude, his ceaseless care of his sheep.

But here, be it noted, in this opening verse, the reference, so direct and unmistakable, is not to an earthly shepherd; it is to the benign and constant Providence of Jehovah toward His children, to the untiring love of God, our Father and Savior, for the souls He has created and redeemed. The psalmist is looking back, in grateful remembrance, upon the history of his race, and upon his own life in particular, and he traces there at every step the goodness and watchfulness of his Creator. He sees there has never been any want. Dark days at times have come upon his nation; sufferings and trials there have been, and in these, as in other respects, his own individual experience has mirrored the history of his people. But throughout it all, there has never been any lasting want. As the shepherd is ever near his sheep, whether at peace or in trouble, to provide for their needs, so, sings the psalmist in gratitude, has God been near him and his people.

And his confidence is unshaken; that which has been in the past will be in the future; as sheep put their trust in their shepherd, so will he put his trust in his Lord and God. And this gratitude for past favors and this unshaken trust for the future is not to be restricted to the psalmist alone. His words had meaning not only for himself; he knows the same Providence provides for us all, and therefore he would have his words find an echo in the hearts and sentiments of all.

∽

You belong to God

The Lord is my Shepherd; He rules me with the rod of gentleness. I am His creation; He has bought me with a great price; He has set me a divine example and taught me the way to life. There may be times of distress for me, brief periods of temporal need; but surely, since I am the possession of my God, and He is providing for me, nothing can long be wanting to me — permanent want there can never be.

The Lord rules me, and all my kind, as a shepherd rules his flock. What a consoling thought to each one of us, if only we be faithful souls! How unspeakable the thought, how surpassing the privilege to know and to be assured that we belong to God, that out of countless millions of creatures, far nobler than we, to whom He might have given the joy of life, He has chosen to select us! To think that He has allotted to us a short period of existence here below, during which it is our privilege to be able to draw near to Him for eternity; and that after this, our little time of trial, we are to reign with Him in everlasting glory!

Of a certainty, we are a favored people and a royal race, for we belong to God. We are His because He created us. He has come down from Heaven to redeem and buy us back from the enemy to whom our race in folly had surrendered itself. He has borne our sorrows and our sufferings to make amends for us and to teach us the way to life. And, finally, He has given His own life for our salvation.

∞

God loved you even before time began
Since, then, God has created us, it follows that He must have had us in His mind from everlasting, because nothing that is, or can be, is unforeseen by Him. From the remotest dawn of eternity, therefore, from the very beginning of the eternal years, He saw us as He sees us now: clearly, distinctly, and lovingly. We did not exist from eternity as we do now, but we were present to God before we were to ourselves; He saw us mirrored in Himself.

And when, in time, He called our race into being and endowed it with life, we know what happened. This human nature of ours, which He had loved from eternity, and favored in time with existence, turned its back upon its God and strayed away to sin and death. This was the disobedience of our first parents, and in their sin we all have shared, for the very reason that they were our parents and were responsible for us as well as for themselves. We became a ruined race, deserving punishment, fit for perdition; and yet God did not give us up. He followed after us, as it were; He pursued us, as a shepherd pursues his chosen flock, until finally He led us back to His fold, and to pastures of rest and plenty.

It was not enough for God's goodness to give us the gift of life and to endow us with understanding, will, and freedom; it did not satisfy His bountifulness to make our life fair here on earth, and to enable us to reap much of the joys and pleasures with which even this world abounds — no, far more than all this has He wished and prepared for His elect, for the souls who belong to His flock. It was nothing less than Himself, Heaven, and its rewards, that the eternal Father had in store for us when He called us into being.

In order, therefore, that we should not lose our destined crowns through the guilt and wounds of Original Sin, He provided for us a remedy: He sent us a Savior, who was His only Son, our Lord Jesus Christ.

Now, since it is to Christ, the Savior, that the spiritual meaning of the shepherd psalm refers in a particular manner, it is in Him especially, and in His earthly life, that we discern and find fulfilled the chief qualities of the good shepherd. As God, we see, He has indeed been our shepherd from the beginning, creating and endowing our nature, and providing for us unnumbered benefits, temporal and eternal. But it is in His human nature, in His character as God and man, that He draws nearest to us and proves to us in ways most gracious that He is, in truth, our loving Master and the Shepherd of our souls. Marvelous, assuredly, has been the goodness of God to create us at all; and still more marvelous that He should have destined us for a participation in His own eternal blessedness; but in no way has the heavenly Father so stooped to us, in no way has He so manifested His utter condescension toward us, as in the abasement of His only-begotten Son, "who, being in the form of God . . . emptied Himself, taking the form of a servant."[6]

Let us reflect that, to raise our race from its fallen state and restore it to the divine good pleasure, it was not necessary for the Second Person of the Most Holy Trinity to have come down to earth. Such extraordinary means were not necessary to bring us back to Heaven's smile and favor. By a simple act of His omnipotent will, God had, in the beginning, called out of nothingness the world and us and all that is. Likewise, by a single wish of the same

---

[6] Phil. 2:6, 7.

divine will, He could have restored us, from a condition of bondage and sin, to the realms of grace and peace.

∞

Christ desired to share human nature

And even when the Son of God did condescend, in accordance with the will of His Father, to clothe Himself with our nature and visit our blighted sphere, how simple He could have made our redemption! How easily He could have blotted out the handwriting that was against us, and presented our tearful world, all smiling and glad, to the arms of His eternal Father! Yes, Christ could have made our redemption easy. He could have paid our debt to God in a thousand different, simple ways, had He wished it so. One drop of His Precious Blood, one tear of His eye, one sigh of His Sacred Heart would have sufficed to redeem innumerable worlds like ours.

But the Savior wished it otherwise. He was our Shepherd, and He loved us, His deceived and wounded sheep. He was with the Father when we were planned and made. He it was, in truth, who made us, for He and the Father are one.[7] He, therefore, knew our nature, since

---

[7] John 10:30, 38, 12:45.

He designed it and gave it to us. He foresaw our yearnings and aspirations; He knew the sublime, transcendent
possibilities of which, with His help and divine example,
we are capable; He understood the heights of love and
worship to which the human heart can ascend, when
assisted from on high; and hence, to awaken and kindle
on earth these all-consuming fires,[8] to stir the very depths
of our souls, and elevate and perfect our gifted nature, to
afford us the utmost inspiration to climb with Him the
heights of Heaven, He stooped to our own estate, in all
things made like unto us, except, indeed, our proneness
and ability to sin.[9] Since He loved us, He longed to be
like us, insofar as that was possible, and not even our
sin-stained, wounded nature could stay the force of His
love.

There is another reason for the mysterious manner
of our redemption, a further explanation of the extreme
condescension on the part of our Lord toward the frail
creatures whom He came to save. Had he come to us in a
foreign attire, with a nature unlike our own, would it not

---

[8] Luke 12:49.
[9] Cf. Phil. 2:7; Heb. 4:15.

have been difficult for us to approach Him and to put our confidence and trust in Him? If He had appeared like an angel, all bright and dazzling with glory, if He had come as an earthly king and ruler, crowned and clad in regal splendor, would it not have been hard for the poor ones of earth? Would it not have been a trial for those who were in need of a shepherd's love and care? Already sorely oppressed and trodden down by worldly pomp and power, they could only have tried to shun His notice and draw back from Him with feelings of fear and awe.

Christ leads by example

But our Redeemer came not only to save, but also to teach and to lead the way to life. As a shepherd, He was not to drive but to lead His sheep; He does not point the direction, but goes before His flock, and they follow Him, and He leads them out to living pastures and to bright, sparkling, far-off waters.

Because He was God, as well as man, Christ knew that, as a result of our sinful state, we would have to pass our earthly sojourn forever beneath the shadow of the cross. When sin entered into the world by the disobedience of the first man, the handiwork of the Creator was despoiled. That which before had been a paradise of pleasure, replete with all delights, was wrecked and ruined, and became a place of sorrow, suffering, and death. Thenceforth, pursuant to the divine decree, the lot of man was to labor, to suffer, and to die.[10] Knowing, therefore, that this was to be our portion, the Shepherd-Savior of our souls must also teach us the secret of pain and toil, and help us to bear our cross.

According, then, to our present state, suffering and sorrow are inseparable from us, because we are born into the world with sin upon our souls and, in the wake of sin, follow all the evils to which the world is heir. And, moreover, under existing conditions, it is necessary for our future happiness that our earthly life be largely spent amid toil and pain and tears. It is only through these that we shall be able to atone for the injuries sin has done, and hold in check the disorders of our nature.

The cross is before us, and we cannot escape it. It is ready for us when we enter the world; it follows us throughout the length of our days, and finally bears us

[10] Gen. 3:19.

down in death to our graves. This does not mean that life on earth is entirely made up of pain and sorrow, for the divine mercy has mitigated even the stroke of sin, and has caused the world, in spite of all its wounds, to bloom with many delights.

Nevertheless, our sojourn here below shall always be fraught with diverse ills, and we at last must yield to death. In spite of all that the world can afford us; in spite of its pleasures and joys, its sunshine and pleasing pastimes, real, though fitful and fast-flying as they are; in spite of health and wealth and fame and honor; in spite of all the goods that life contains — it still is ever true that we live in a region of tears, and that death and sorrow are sure to follow upon the footsteps of joy and mirth. It must be so, for the stains of sin are indelibly upon the world, and not until God establishes "the new Heaven and the new earth"[11] can life on earth be made entirely happy.

All this our Savior knew when He chose our human nature and embraced a life of labor and sorrow. His divine foreknowledge took in our lives, and the lives of all our

[11] Cf. Rev. 21:1.

kind, until the end of all shall be. Our infant tears, our trials and pains of body, the ceaseless pangs of mind and heart that pursue us throughout life, were all before Him as in a mirror, and He had to instruct and assist us to fight this battle and walk this way of earth, lest all should perish before the journey's end.

Since we were to suffer, He would suffer also. Since our lives were to be amid labors and trials, He would labor and travail also. Since we were to feel the sting of pain, be subject to heat and cold, be in want, in poverty, and in distress, be misunderstood, be thwarted, be cast down from our highest hopes, and broken, at times, in every cheerful prospect — since these and other countless ills were to be woven into our web of earthly life, He, the divine Master, who came to save, to teach a lesson, to suffer and die, would assume a body so sacred, so delicate, so pure and sensitive that, when exposed to the rough and ruthless ways of life, He could truly cry out from the depths of His anguish: "O all ye that pass by the way, attend and see if there be any sorrow like unto my sorrow!"[12]

---

[12] Lam. 1:12.

∽

Christ is with you in your sufferings

How comforting, then, it is for us to feel that we are not alone in suffering, and to know that, while all we suffer is just and due to our sinful state, we can nevertheless make use of all our ills to attain to joys unending in Heaven! If we must toil and struggle while on earth, it is because these things are a result of our state; if we must be subject to sickness, to weakness and fatigue, to cold and hunger, to weariness and pain, it is not because God is pleased at the misery of His creatures, and neither does He rejoice on account of our misfortune. We are simply reaping the harvest of sin and transgression, and sin is the work of our own free choice and that of our ancestors.

And even though it may be objected that we are born into this inevitable condition, and are made the unconsulted heirs of a heritage we loathe but cannot escape, the solution to our difficulty is not far to seek. We need but hearken to the promptings of reason, and lift our sorrowing eyes to the realms of faith to be convinced that God's mercy and goodness are above all His works,[13] and

---

[13] Ps. 144:9 (RSV = Ps. 145:9).

that, for reasons no less benevolent than holy, He has called us into life and permitted all our woes. God could not have created us for suffering and punishment, because He is infinite goodness; He cannot be pleased at our misfortunes, since He Himself has borne our sorrows and carried all our pains.[14] If He Himself had not come into the world in visible human form, if He had not explained our purpose and destiny, and led the way to Heaven, if He had not, by His words and divine example, provided us with the solution for all of life's difficulties, then, in truth, we might object, and sit and grieve and wonder. But in the light of the life of Christ, all this is altered; the picture takes on a different coloring.

Who, now, can think of the sufferings of Christ and rail at the crosses of life? Who can remember the Passion of Jesus and murmur at the injustice of pain? Who can look upon the Savior dying and say that God is deaf to our pleading and unmoved by our tears? Who can recall the price that was paid for our souls and ponder the death of our God and believe that our lives are of little worth, or of no account with the Almighty?

[14] Isa. 53:4.

Thus it is with a bountiful goodness that the Savior has purchased His sheep. By His own free choice, by a life of entirely voluntary suffering, endured for our salvation and instruction, through a bitter but willing agony and death, He has provided the means to free us from sin, and has bequeathed to us every blessing. Now we can truly say, "The Lord is my shepherd; I shall not want." If only we can look into that divine life which has been given as our model, if only we can ponder it, and read in it the lessons, the hopes, and the inspirations it contains for us, we shall not be weary of our burdens and cares; we shall not falter in any of life's battles. Rather, rejoicing at our opportunities, eternal as they are, and with feelings of exultant gratitude over our condition, as heirs with Christ to the kingdom of Heaven,[15] we shall bravely welcome all the conflicts of life, being assured with St. Paul that "this slight momentary affliction is preparing for us an eternal weight of glory."[16]

[15] Rom. 8:17.
[16] 2 Cor. 4:17 (RSV).

Chapter Four

The eucharistic Christ brings your soul rest

∞

"He maketh me to lie down
in pastures of tender grass;
He leadeth me beside
the waters of quietness."

Our attention is now directed to a particular phase of the shepherd's life, and here we see some of the ways in which he actually provides for the sheep day by day. For it is not enough for the shepherd to have purchased his flock, by means however difficult and labors however loving; it is not sufficient for him to have procured for them, in a general manner, all that they need for their life and safety; he must also arrange for their daily care and provide for their separate wants.

Sheep, as we know, are delicate creatures, and they must be directed in their roamings, and sustained by sufficient nourishment. Accordingly, we have said that it belongs to the duties of a good shepherd to lead them out to pasture, and to provide adequate food and drink for them every day.

Here again we behold the infinite kindness of the Shepherd of our souls. Not only has He deigned to stoop to our fallen state and restore us from death to life, not only did He take upon Himself our infirmities and bear our woes, but He has also tenderly provided for our constant direction, and for the daily needs of our lives.

The level to which the Savior raised our lives and the dignity to which He invites us are far, indeed, above our natural powers. Left to ourselves, we could never attain the heavenly heights to which, in His goodness, He has called us. Through the infinite merits of His life and sacrifice, we have been redeemed and reclaimed from the enemy of our souls. The gates of Heaven, closed against us before, have been opened wide, and our wayward race is again restored to the road that leads to our immortal home.

But just because our celestial destiny is of so high and sublime a character, it is impossible, if left to our own abilities, for us to pursue it for long, and vastly beyond our sublimest hopes that we should ever finally attain it. We have, it is true, ever before us, the life and example of

Him who has saved us; we know that His Cross and death have delivered us from the wrath that frowned upon us. But we are weak and fragile mortals. With respect to things of the higher life — of the supernatural world — we, of ourselves, shall always remain as helpless and frail as infants. No less unable is the babe of yesterday to traverse unaided and explore the material world, than the wisest of men would be to know and grasp by his natural powers the unrevealed good of the immortal human spirit. And as, in our natural state, we could not know the true end of our existence without divine Revelation, so likewise, we could not pursue and attain our spiritual destiny without special assistance from on high.

Christ teaches and strengthens you

How well all this was known to our kind and kingly Shepherd! How keenly did He appreciate our frailty and inability to walk along the paths which He had trodden! Therefore, He constantly taught and directed the way which leads to unending life. When going before his flock and teaching them by example, He did not neglect to give them that saving doctrine which, when He had disappeared, would be their guide, and the guide to their future shepherds in the direction of safety and truth. Hence He propounded a teaching which should be to its obedient followers a realization at once of all He had promised them, and of all their hearts' desires. It is not that it would make them rich or great in the eyes of the world and according to human standards, but that it would confer a truer and higher greatness by lifting them above their weak and natural level and preparing them for eternal blessedness.

Men had the Law before the coming of Christ; they knew the Ten Commandments. But the state to which the God-Man called them, and the eminence to which they were raised, were quite beyond anything the world until then had ever been able to conceive. Human nature, under the New Covenant, was invited to attain to perfection. Things which before were thought impossible were now to be the objects of our daily strivings. It was no longer "an eye for an eye, and a tooth for a tooth";[17] now good was to be done not only to those who were good to us, but also to those who did us evil; we were not only to love our friends, but also to love and assist

[17] Exod. 21:24; Matt. 5:38.

our enemies.[18] Not only should evil deeds be avoided, but evil thoughts were likewise forbidden.[19] Yes, we were asked to be, in all our thoughts and deeds, imitators of the Shepherd who leads us.[20]

Poor human nature, when raised so high above its natural powers, stood in perilous need of a shepherd's tender care. The new demands of every day made new and special daily helps indispensable. While our spirits can see and know the way under the light of heavenly teaching, yet how weak and faltering is our flesh! We have the will to do; but to accomplish, we alone are not able. Therefore our Savior said, "Of yourselves, you can do nothing, but in me all things are possible to you. The branches are nothing unless they abide in the vine; I am the vine, you the branches."[21]

Thus He is our Leader, our divine Teacher, and our source of strength. Without Him we can do nothing, but in Him we are strong. And daily and constantly He is near us, although we see Him not. It is He who sustains

[18] Matt. 5:44.
[19] Matt. 5:28.
[20] Cf. Matt. 5:48.
[21] John 15:4-5.

our very life and moves us to all that is good. Like an ever-present friend, He offers us constant assistance; He instructs and guides and helps us, and this is the strength and food of our souls. It is God's grace, always ready for our use, which makes possible all the high demands put upon our nature. Without it we would faint and starve on our journey, and hence He who has planned our high perfection has provided the help to attain it.

What are those seven wonderful sacraments which He has left us, but perennial channels of grace, constant fountains from which stream the life-giving waters that nourish our weary souls and make them strong for life eternal? Through these sacred means, we are brought into contact with the life and merits of our Shepherd-Redeemer. They prolong His life and labors among us; they continue in our midst the strength of His sacred presence.

The Eucharist calls for faith

In a manner altogether special is this true of the holy sacrament of the altar. By the Holy Eucharist, Christ still is with us, and will so remain until the end of time, as really and as truly as He dwelt on earth in the days of His mortal life.

Bound as we are by the things of sense, we may, at times, be tempted to complain that Christ in this sacrament is all invisible to us. We cannot see Him directly and immediately. His voice is silent, and we do not hear Him; we do not feel the caress of His hand. But nevertheless we know He is present, for He has said it, and His word must remain, even if Heaven and earth should pass away.[22] Even were we privileged to see the sacred humanity as it was seen of old in Palestine, we would not then, more than now in this sacrament, directly see the divinity concealed by the human frame. Faith was required then as well as now — faith in His sacred words, made evident by His sacred deeds.

This is not strange; it is not too much to ask. The same demand of faith is daily made upon us in much of our interchanges with our fellow mortals. Much that we do not clearly see we must perforce believe, or else life would be impossible. The same, in a measure, is true in all our human friendships. That which is most precious in our friends, that which is the source of life and beauty, of holy words and loving actions, of all we love and

[22] Cf. Matt. 24:35.

cherish in them, is the soul, the spirit that quickens and moves — and this we do not see.

Thus Christ in the Eucharist is truly present, although faith alone can understand Him. He requires of us this faith — this humble subjection of our sensible faculties to the power and truth of His words. It is all for our good that now He is hidden from our sight. He is no less truly present, no less truly kind, no less loving, no less merciful and forbearing; but He wishes to exercise our faith, to prove our fidelity and trust in His teaching and promises, and hence He is hidden from the powers of our senses.

In the sacrament of the Eucharist, the gracious Shepherd of our souls performs in particular three offices for us: He is our sacrifice; our silent, patient friend; and, in Communion, the actual spiritual food of our souls.

∞

Christ offers Himself as a sacrifice

As a victim, Christ is daily and constantly, from the rising to the setting of the sun, lifted up for us in the Holy Sacrifice of the Mass. The Mass is the perpetuation of the sacrifice He offered long ago for our redemption. All the altars throughout the world, on which He is ever born and dies again in mystical repetition, are but an

extension of the one great altar of Calvary, where first
He gave His life for our salvation.

And in this real and awe-inspiring sacrifice, forever
repeated in our midst, He again pleads our cause with God,
the eternal Father. Again in a mystical manner He suffers
for us, again He bleeds, again He is nailed to the Cross
and raised on high, and in that same abandoned, pitiable
state to which His love for His flock has reduced Him, ever
in our behalf He pleads, "Father, forgive them, for they
know not what they do![23] Holy Father, powerful God, stay
Thy avenging hand, and save the souls which Thou hast
created for Thyself, and for which until the end of time I
die!" He lifts, as it were, before the great white throne,
His bruised and blood-stained hands; He shows those
wounded feet, the scar of the spear in His sacred side; He
points again to the agony in the garden, to the scourging
at the pillar, to the cruel crown of thorns, to the weary
way of the Cross, and exclaims to Him who sits upon
the throne, "Behold, my Father, and see the price of my
sheep, the tears and sorrow and blood they have cost me!
And spare them and save them for the sake of Thy Son!"

[23] Luke 23:34.

Through the Holy Sacrifice of the Mass, identical as it is with the sacrifice of Calvary, all the merits of Christ's life and death are applied to our souls. By His physical and bloody immolation on Calvary, Christ purchased for us infinite treasures of grace, and it is His will that these graces shall be dispensed to us, even until the end of the world, through the August sacrament of the altar.

Moreover, except for the Mass, we would not be blessed with the abiding actual presence of our divine Shepherd among us — that is, we would not possess Him in that special, intimate manner in which we now have Him in the Eucharist. For it is only in the Mass that the Sacred Species are consecrated; and consequently it is through the Mass alone that He takes up His sacramental presence in our midst and becomes our food in Holy Communion. He could, indeed, have ordained it otherwise, but such has been His blessed will, and such is the condition in which we are placed by the direction of His holy Church.

∞

Christ is your abiding Friend

Besides being our daily sacrifice, then, under the appearance of bread and wine, besides ever prolonging in

our midst that wondrous act of Calvary by which at once
He liberated our race and reopened to us the gates of
Heaven, the bounteous Shepherd of our souls enters into
the tabernacles of our churches, and there, in silent, patient waiting, He craves the love of our hearts and longs
for our intimate friendship. He is not content merely to
plead for us with God, His Father; He is not content continually to renew in our presence the tragic mystery by
which, at the end of His earthly labors, He procured for
us every blessing — no, over and above these sovereign
acts of kindest benediction, He wishes to remain among
us, and to converse with us, each and all, as a friend
would converse with his friend. This is what He meant
when He said by the mouth of His inspired writer, "My
delights are to be with the children of men."[24]

As a Shepherd, His chief pleasure, as well as His
supreme care, is to be with the flock He has purchased
and loves. Yet it is a lonely life for our Shepherd-King,
this abode in the silent tabernacle, but it is all for love
of us. He wishes to be there where we can find Him,
where we can come to Him at any hour and speak to

[24] Prov. 8:31.

Him, to praise and thank Him for all His dear and end-
less gifts, to tell Him our needs and our sorrows, to open
our breaking hearts to Him and reveal the secrets of our
souls. It is this that He desires from us — the outpouring
of our hearts and souls in His presence. It is this which
renders unto Him that homage of faith and love and
devotion that He came into the world to inspire.

It will not do to say that, being God, He is acquainted
with all our thoughts and aware of all our wants, for it is
intimacy and confidence that He desires — the intimacy
and confidence which alone can create a true and noble
friendship. "I will no longer call you servants," He said
to His disciples, "but I have called you friends; the servant knoweth not what his master doth, but a friend is
admitted to confidence."[25] Christ in the tabernacle is our
friend; He has loved us unto the end, and He yearns for
our love in return.

Why is this? Why are we so precious in His eyes?
What are we, that the great Creator should at all be
mindful of us?[26]

[25] Cf. John 15:15.
[26] Cf. Ps. 8:5 (RSV = Ps. 8:4).

We must remember and ever bear in mind the lofty purpose which the Creator had in view when first He called us into being — the same purpose which prompted our redemption and all the gracious dispensations that have followed thereupon — namely, that God, while achieving His own eternal honor and glory, might communicate to us a portion of His own ineffable blessedness. We were made for God, and not for the world or for creatures or for ourselves. And precisely because we are the possession and property of God, He wants us, soul and body, for Himself. In the Blessed Sacrament, He calls to us individually, "Son, give me thy heart."[27] "Come to me, all you who are burdened, and I will refresh you. . . . Come to me and find rest for your souls; I will lead you beside the waters of quietness."[28]

∞

Christ is the food of your soul

But the excesses of our Shepherd's love and care do not stop with the altar and with the tabernacle. He is not satisfied with being our daily sacrifice and our abiding

---

[27] Prov. 23:26.
[28] Cf. Matt. 11:28; Ps. 22:2 (RSV = Ps. 23:2).

Friend, not satisfied until He enters into our very bosom and unites us to Himself. Union with the beloved object and delight in its presence are characteristic of all true friendship, whether human or divine. That which we really love, we desire to have, to possess, to be united with; and hence it is that Christ, the lover of our souls, has not only given His life to purchase us for Himself and Heaven, but has so extended His loving kindness as to become Himself our actual food.

It is incomprehensible, in a human way, that the love of a shepherd for his flock, the love of God for His creatures, should be so extraordinary as to provide the wondrous benefits which Christ in the Eucharist has wrought for us. We simply cannot grasp with our feeble minds the prodigality of such enduring love. But the Savior knew His purpose with us, and He knew the needs of our souls.

As guests destined for an eternal banquet, and as heirs to celestial thrones, it is needful for us, amid the rough ways and perils of life, to be constantly reminded of our royal destiny and strengthened against our daily foes. This world of ours is an arena in which each one must contend for his eternal prize; and it is not possible, considering our natural frailty and the enemies that oppose our forward march, that we alone, without added strength, should ever be able to win the battle of life. Hence, as the body, to maintain its vigor and perform its work, needs its material and earthly food, so the soul, to live and be strong, must be nourished with the bread of Heaven. "The bread that I will give," said our Lord, "is my flesh for the life of the world. . . . Unless you eat of this bread you cannot have life in you. He that eateth my flesh and drinketh my blood hath life everlasting, and I will raise him up on the last day."[29]

In order, then, to sustain our spiritual life on earth and to make us strong for our daily conflicts, our heavenly Shepherd has left us a food which is none other than His own Body and Blood. What a prodigy of love! What could He do for us that He has not done?

But, besides giving us strength, He had another purpose in becoming our food. Since He has chosen us for Himself, and has provided, in another world, eternal mansions for our souls,[30] He wishes to make certain, not

[29] John 6:52, 54-55 (RSV = John 6:51, 53-54).
[30] John 14:2.

only the happy issue of our lives, but our ever-increasing resemblance to Him. He is therefore preparing us; He is fitting us, through communion in the Holy Eucharist, for our celestial home, and for visible companionship with Him. Communion, intimate relationship, produces likeness, even here on earth, and it is a singular effect of Holy Communion that, unlike earthly food, it changes into itself all those who partake of it. Material, natural food becomes the substance of our flesh and blood, but frequent participation in the heavenly nourishment of Christ in the Eucharist transmutes our whole being — our lives and thoughts and actions — into its own supernatural character.

Thus, by living much with Christ on earth, by intimate converse with Him, by allowing Him to enter into our lives and thoughts and to shape our conduct and actions, and, above all, by frequent and fervent communion with Him in the sacrament of His love, we become like Him, even here in our state of exile. And this likeness to Christ, which His faithful servants assume here below, is a foretaste of future blessedness; it is a preparation for the great reunion and the eternal banquet which await us in Heaven.

Christ brings your soul rest

Already we are led beside the waters of rest; we are directed to pastures of sweetest nourishment; and through the calm and vigor that reign in the soul, we experience even now a taste of joys unseen.

Chapter Five

Christ the Good Shepherd
heals and forgives

∞

"He restores my soul."

Throughout the pastoral country of the Orient, there are numerous places of great peril for sheep. There are also, here and there, private fields and vineyards and gardens into which, if a member of a flock should stray and be caught, it is forfeited to the owner of the land. Strange as it may seem, the sheep never learn to avoid these dangerous spots and forbidden places, and it behooves the shepherd to be ever on his guard for them, and to rescue them when they are wandering.

Here we cannot fail to observe the striking resemblance between this wayward tendency of the shepherd's flock and our own inclination and propensity to wander from God and from things eternal. The world is full of

occasions to evil; at every turn of the road on our journey
through life, there are fierce and crouching enemies
awaiting the chance to capture us and bear us away.
We know this. We have often been warned of the danger. Too many sad experiences and breathless escapes
have convinced us of the sundry perils to soul and body
that lie along the way of life. But we, like senseless, erring
sheep, if bereft of the Shepherd's guiding care, do not
learn, in life's sad school, the way to keep free from harm.
Although wounded repeatedly, scarred and worn, and
left, perhaps, without human aid, to waste and bleed our
life away, we do not see the lurking evils; we do not discern beneath the mask the enemy whose purpose is ruin
and death.

The creatures of the world and the things of sense
take vicious hold of us, and often drag us to the very
verge of perdition before we are aware. They catch us
unprepared, seek entrance into our lives and thoughts,
and allure us by deception. They tell us that the world is
fair and beautiful and full of promise; that God, for the
moment, is not concerned; that the soul is secure and
safe, and the body and its needs are the only object of
present solicitude.

Ambition, pride, pleasure, and the like are deceivers that plunder and sack their victims' goods. And when these painted idols of a passing world have led away their worshipers as slaves, and stripped them of all they possessed, they give them over to evil habits and to masters that scourge and tear them. Like other prodigals, these pursuers of earthly phantoms take leave of their Father's house of comfort and plenty; they give up virtue, innocence, honesty, and purity; they go into a far country to waste their substance living riotously, only to awake, too soon, to a land of famine, and to find themselves alone and in want. Instead of the honor and fame and high estate they sought to gain, instead of the escape from evil and pain and labor they hoped to find, they are sent into fields to minister to swine — the swine of their own degradation.[31]

So, to a degree, it is with us, each and all, who listen to other voices and heed other calls than the voice and the call of God. If we prefer to stray to other fields and desert the pasture of our Shepherd, if we prefer a far country to our Father's home, if the world and its fleeting pleasures

---

[31] Cf. Luke 15:11-16.

are more to us than God and His paternal rewards, then
we must of necessity find ourselves at length in utter
want and penury.

It is this possibility of deserting God, of seeking happiness outside of Him, of overturning the plans which He
has made for our salvation, that gives us a vision of the
awful failure of human life. The gifts of this world are by
nature fleeting and fast-flying, and if we allow them to
take the place of Him who made them, no matter how
great our present boons, in spite of wealth and friends
and all success, we have missed our chance and our purpose in the world, and can only have at last a desolate
and ruined life.

But how is it, then, one may ask, that man can be
so deceived? How is it that we do not learn from others'
disasters to avoid those deceiving, ruinous masters, those
false gods that can lead us away from the one true Shepherd of our souls?

It is, indeed, a curious fact that our deception is so
easy. Surely a rational, intelligent being who stops to
consider should easily be able to distinguish between the
great God of Heaven and the creatures of His hands. It
should not be difficult for us to see the transient vanity

of human things when compared with the eternal mansions.[32]

∞

Man's fallen nature and sinfulness lead him astray

But the truth of the matter is that we are deceived; we do not at all times see the objects of our choice as they really are objectively. Our vision is defective and blurred. If God stood out in our lives as He really ought to, if He occupied that place in our thoughts and plans which belongs to Him by right, it would not be possible that we should ever be led astray. And that God does not always hold in our lives the place which is His due is partly the result of our fallen nature — partly, therefore, in a way, excusable — but more frequently and chiefly it is from our own perversity, from willful neglect of our highest duties.

The blindness and perversity of our nature, which have come from the wounds of Original Sin, make it easy for us, if we are neglectful and careless of our higher spiritual obligations, to mistake the false for the true, evil for good, the creature for the Creator. In the midst of the

[32] Luke 16:9.

world and its allurements, it behooves us to be ever watching, if we are never to stumble and to fall. Had our nature never been corrupted by original unfaithfulness, had our first parents never turned away from God and transgressed His sacred precept, all our present ills would never have existed. But now it is different. We are born into the world a weakened people; each one of us has had an implicit part in the first transgression; we all, like erring sheep, have gone astray.[33]

And while this tendency to evil is part of our natural condition, and therefore less imputable to us, it nevertheless is true that our actual sins and evildoing are the work of our deliberate choice. If, at any time, we really turn away from God and break His law, it is because we have freely chosen so to act. It is true that a weak and wounded nature leaves one less able to choose what is right, and more disposed to wrong, but the native perversity of nature in a normal man can never explain or excuse the grievous sins which he deliberately commits.

And because we know the state of things, because we know that the fault is really ours when we dare to stray to

---

[33] Isa. 53:6.

forbidden deeds and places, how constant and unrelenting, if we are truly wise, should be our efforts to keep our vision unobscured and our ears attuned to the voice and call of our heavenly Shepherd! We know that, if we follow Him, our way will be certain and clear. Howsoever enormous the evils of life, and notwithstanding all our weakness, we know that in Him we are safe and strong. But we must hear Him to follow Him; we must be guided and directed by His gracious commands.

This failure to hear and obey the voice of God explains the falls and sins of men better than does all their inherited frailty. So long as God's words are heard and His directions heeded, mistake and error are impossible. We see, therefore, why it is that so many actually do desert Him and are led by evil voices. The cause lies chiefly in the willfulness of human nature and in the abuse of human liberty. We cannot stand unless God supports us, and we shall surely fall if He withdraws His supporting hand. But the choice of evil, the beginning of unfaithfulness, comes from ourselves; for Almighty God will never forsake us unless we first forsake Him.

If ever, then, we find our lives to be at variance with God, whether in lesser or in greater matters, if it should

ever be our unhappy fortune to wander from Him, like
another prodigal, and waste our lives with the enemies
of our souls, we can be assured that the desertion is all
our own. We forget God, we deliberately wander from
His sight and care, and then we fall. Engrossed in worldly
affairs, taken up with present vanities, with ourselves, our
ease, and our temporal advancement, we begin to neglect
prayer and communion with God, we begin to rely on
ourselves and to forge ahead of our own accord, only
to encounter complete defeat and be shorn of all our
strength. The secret of our power and success is to keep
close to Him, to speak to Him lovingly and often, to seek
guidance and protection from Him, and habitually to live
in His comforting presence.

∞

Christ seeks straying souls

But such is the boundless kindness of our heavenly
Shepherd that, no matter how often we may have wandered from Him, or how seriously we may have grieved
Him, He is ever ready to pursue our wanderings, and to
seek until He finds us. He does not stop to consider the
enormity of our guilt, or our unreasonableness, or our in-
gratitude, but He seeks us. He does not pause to take an

account of all He has done for us, of the many graces He has given us, of the tears and blood He has shed in our behalf; but He goes after our straying souls, and He will not be appeased until He restore us. God does not will the death of the sinner, but that he be converted and live.[34] He knows all our frailties and our diverse temptations; He knows how alluring are the things of sense to a nature perverted like ours; He knows how easy it is for us, blind and ignorant as we are, to forget Him and our dearest interests, and to obey the call of other voices. All this He understands, and He has pity on us. "He knoweth our frame, He remembereth that we are dust."[35]

To bring us back, therefore, when we are wandering, and to restore us to the circle of His chosen flock, our Savior has made ample provision. Through those divine mediums of grace — the sacraments of His Church — He has arranged to provide for all our wants and to cure our various infirmities. The sacraments of Baptism and Penance, in particular, were instituted to raise our souls from death to life, and to heal our spiritual wounds.

[34] Ezek. 33:11; 2 Pet. 3:9.
[35] Ps. 102:14 (RSV = Ps. 103:14).

∞

Baptism is the entry into Christ's fold

Baptism may be aptly compared to the door of the sheepfold. It is the gate through which men must enter into the fold of Christ; it is the entrance to His Church. It clears away the guilt and stain of Original Sin and restores the soul from a state of enmity to the friendship and grace of God. None can really belong to Christ, none can be of His true fold, who have not entered by way of the door, who have not been baptized. Many there are who pretend to belong to Him and think themselves of the number of His flock. They speak of Him as their Master and Shepherd; they pretend to be doing His work; they call Him Lord and preach in His name; but they have not entered by the door of the sheepfold, and He knows them not. Like thieves and robbers, they have climbed up some other way, and they do not know Him, nor does He know them, nor can they understand His voice. Baptism is the entrance, the door, to the fold of Christ.

∞

Penance calls you back to Christ

And as it is through Baptism that our bountiful Lord first recalls us from the ways of sin and makes us members of His flock, so, in the sacrament of Penance, He has provided a means by which we may at all times be recalled from our wanderings and restored to His friendship. Penance is an inexhaustible means of reconciliation between the erring soul and God. It lasts throughout our lives; it stretches even to the end of time. If only we are men of goodwill and have at heart our eternal interests, we need not be disturbed at our frailty, or at repeated lapses into sin. There is no sin which cannot be forgiven by the sacrament of Penance. This is not to say that anyone, knowing that he can be forgiven, should presume to abuse God's gracious sacrament, and yield freely and without restraint to the voice of sin, nor that we are not to be truly sorry to the end of our days for having even once offended our benign Maker and Redeemer. But we must be confident that, whatever may have been our faults and failings, however prolonged and extraordinary our transgressions, if we approach the sacrament of Penance with sincere sorrow and a firm purpose of amendment, God will always lovingly receive us back to Himself, and remember no more our unfaithfulness.

God hates sin, because it is opposed to Him and is the only evil in the world, but He loves the wounded sinner who is made in His own image and likeness. Precious in the sight of God is the penitent sinner. Does He not tell us Himself that, like a good shepherd, He leaves ninety-nine just to go in search of one lost sheep? Yes, He assures us that there is rejoicing among the angels of Heaven over one sinner who does penance.[36]

To make worthy use of the sacrament of Penance, we must be truly sorry for having offended God, and be resolved, at the time of confession, to do what lies in our power never again to turn away from Him. To these dispositions must also be joined the intention of doing something to repair the injury which sin has done to God. Given such conditions, we need only speak the word to God's duly appointed minister and our sins are no more. The dark veil which hung around our soul like a cloud is lifted, and we again rejoice in the smile of our heavenly Father.

How simple, yet how potent are the means provided for our salvation! None but God could have thought of them, nothing but the love of God could have arranged them!

[36] Luke 15:4, 7.

But even before the sinner is brought to penance, even while he is wandering and reveling afar off in the vile delights of sin, God is pursuing him, seeking after him, calling him by name, whispering to his heart, and disposing him for repentance. Once we have deserted Him, we cannot return to God without His help. It is our awful power to be able to leave Him, but to return by ourselves we are not able. Wherefore He comes after us when we have wandered into the wilds of sin; He pleads, as it were, with our souls and offers us the grace to repent.

Oh, privileged are our souls to be thus appraised by God, and happy those who hear and heed the appealing voice of His grace!

Chapter Six

Christ's Church guards you from spiritual dangers

∞

"He leads me in the
paths of justice
for His Name's sake."

The shepherd country of the East is full of walks and pathways, some leading this way, some that. Some lead to dangerous precipices over which the sheep might fall and be lost, others would expose them to the attack of wild beasts, while still others would lead them so far astray that they would not be able to find their way back. It is, therefore, always needful that the shepherd go ahead of his flock and lead them in the right path.

The psalmist applies this carefulness of the shepherd for his sheep to our Lord, in His regard for our spiritual welfare. The Savior goes before us with the blessings of His goodness to help and lead us aright, lest perchance we become lost and perish in our journey.

This solicitude of our Redeemer in providing for the various needs of our souls is characteristic of Him as Savior. It is implied in the meaning of His name. Before He was born, before He was conceived in His Mother's womb, it was foretold of Him that He should be called Jesus, which means Savior, for He would save His people from their sins.[37] He exercised, as we know, this mission of Savior throughout His earthly career. It was for this that He came into the world; for this that He was born in Bethlehem with a manger as His cradle; for this that, at the age of twelve, He was found teaching in the Temple; for this that He retired to Nazareth and was subject to Mary and Joseph; for this that He labored and suffered and bled and died.

∞

Christ guides you on life's road

And with His passing from this visible scene to the bosom of His Father, He did not cease to be that for which He had been eternally anointed — the great High Priest, the Mediator between God and man, the Savior of the world. His work is everlasting, and now that He has

---

[37] Matt. 1:21.

gone up on high, He pleads for us evermore with the Father. We belong to Him, He has purchased us with His blood, and He must care for our safety to the end.

Inasmuch as we are heirs, according to divine decree, to thrones beyond the skies, it was necessary, as we have seen, that He who is our Savior and Shepherd should have left behind Him in this world of ours a doctrine, a code or system of instructions and laws, which should safely direct and guide us to our royal destiny. Those who lived with Him on earth, those who heard His assuring, life-giving words, and felt the inspiration of His example and visible presence had no need to fear for the direction or safety of their course. They enjoyed the divine, living voice and sacred presence of their Lord and Master, and care and anxiety fled from their souls.

And not for these alone had the Redeemer come, but for all mankind — for all who, in the future, were to breathe the breath of human life. He came to save all; He died for all; and thus the teaching which He gave to the world, and which He committed to His chosen followers, was for every human being, even to the end of the world, so that, through it, all might live and attain to life everlasting.

The doctrine which the Savior left us, and the laws which He prescribed were vastly different from the teachings of men. Guiding, saving words of a Shepherd to His flock, they engendered safety, comfort, and peace. Free from error or mistake, sealed with the seal of Heaven, holding out a promise of future glory, they exhaled the perfumes of the eternal city; they told of mansions not built with hands.

And since this immaculate doctrine, given for the souls of men, was to last until the end of time, there was need that it should be shielded against the assaults of the world and protected from the influence of our changing human teachings. It could not be corrected, because it contained no mistakes; it could not be changed or altered, because it came from the changeless God; it could have no substitute from the part of men or creatures of any kind, because it was given by Him who alone was the way, the truth, and the life.[38] Consequently, the truths which the Savior declared to the world as the only means by which we can be saved, were at once infallible in themselves, and so provided for that no human agency, no lapse of

---

[38] John 14:6.

years or revolutions of time and place should ever be able to infringe on their eternal, changeless character.

∞

Christ's Church guards His flock

It was to preserve these truths in their integrity and freshness that He founded His unerring Church and committed to her the office of custodian and expounder, under the guidance of His Holy Spirit, of all He had revealed for the salvation of humankind. Hence, to hear our Shepherd's voice, to understand what He says to us, to know what we must do to obey His laws and save our souls, we need but listen to the voice of His Church. Before it was established, He declared that He would build His Church upon a rock, and that no enemy, or group of enemies, and not even the gates of Hell would ever prevail against her.[39] He established the Church as His mouthpiece, and He said to the little band that constituted the Church in the beginning: "He that heareth you, heareth me, and he that heareth me, heareth Him that sent me."[40] And, as if to emphasize this declaration,

[39] Matt. 16:18.
[40] Luke 10:16.

He added that anyone who would not hear and obey the Church should be considered as a heathen and a publican.[41] The Church, therefore, is the oracle of God; she is His mouthpiece; she possesses and guards the only revelation which God has made to His rational creatures; she alone has the words of eternal life.

Thus it is that our divine Shepherd goes before us, leading us in the paths of truth and justice, preserving us from danger and error with respect to our spiritual destiny. We cannot go astray if we listen to Him speaking to us through His Church. In all our perplexities and uncertainties, when confronted by any doubt, or confused and distracted by the wrangling voices and conflicting opinions of men, we can be calm and at peace, assured in our inmost souls that the voice which guides us cannot err, that it is easier for Heaven and earth to pass away than for one word of His to fail.[42]

"He leads me in paths of justice," in the ways of holiness, in the ways which the saints have walked. How exceedingly great, indeed, is our privilege, and how certain

[41] Matt. 18:17.
[42] Cf. Matt. 24:35.

and individual our election! All that remains for us is to listen to His words and to follow Him, and present peace will attend our labors, while future glory will wait upon our end.

But in the midst of the abundant blessings and spiritual favors which have surrounded and sheltered us from infancy, we are apt to be unmindful of our state of plenty and forgetful of the duty of gratitude. We are apt to venture out like thoughtless children, trusting in our own strength to battle with the foe; or else, on the contrary, we sluggishly presume that a bountiful Providence will provide for us regardless of our own cooperation. We have never known what it is to want for spiritual food and spiritual direction, except when indolence, careless indifference, and our own folly have led us astray. These are evils which continually assail us, and we often make friends with them, not knowing what we are doing for the most part, until the blood of life has almost ebbed away.

∽

False teachers seek to lead you astray
We are not, indeed, removed from a world where sin abounds and where deceiving voices may lure us this way

and that. Like the pastoral country of the Orient, the walks of life are fraught with perils: false teachers, false doctrines, false prophets, pseudo-christs;[43] perils from our own nation, and perils from abroad, perils in the city and perils in the wilderness, perils in the sea and perils from false brethren"[44] — all trying to attract us and lead us away from the paths of justice and deliver us to the enemy of our souls.

It is necessary that we should know that wolves are abroad in sheep's clothing — "false apostles, deceitful workers, transforming themselves into the apostles of Christ."[45] They come to us with winning words and easy teachings, with new creeds, new forms of belief, and new ways to the promised land. The doctrine and truths which Christ taught and which He entrusted to His Church are set aside or explained away by these modern teachers, and the novel and the strange are made to assume the role of the old, the familiar, and the true.

The harm done is incalculable. How many innocent and unwary sheep have been lost to the fold of Christ by

[43] Matt. 24:24.
[44] 2 Cor. 11:26.
[45] 2 Cor. 11:13.

following the call of these unworthy preachers and false shepherds! What multitudes of precious souls have been deceived by their polished words and led away into paths of error, into deadly ways of thinking, believing, and acting, never to return to the path that leads to life!

This poisoning of the soul and the heart by erroneous doctrines is effected in many and diverse ways; the victims of falsehood are variously captured. The wisdom and sagacity of men, the conquests of science and the learning of the philosophers, the discoveries of our day, the strides of history, the breakdown and overthrow of many things held sacred by our forefathers — all these changes and ruptures in the order of a former generation are now used to beguile the flock of Christ and sway them from the paths of truth and righteousness.

Christ speaks through His Church

But amid all this din and uproar of conflicting voices, amid the wrangling tumult and confusion of converging opinions, those who will may hear and discern the loving voice of the true Shepherd speaking to the world through His Church with the same calm, assuring words which He uttered to living witnesses two thousand years ago.

He has not changed, nor has His teaching. He has not deserted His chosen flock, but is with it all days, even to the end of the world.[46] In spite of our enemies, His love for us, His watchfulness for our needs, and His enduring care for our interests can never fail.

And while assured of this, it behooves us, out of gratitude and to awaken a greater love of Him, to reflect that this abiding faithfulness of our Savior in caring for our wants is not from any worthiness of ours, or because of our merits, but only for His Name's sake, because He is Savior. It was His love for us that prompted our creation, that provoked His Passion and redeemed us, that made Him suffer for us, that teaches and shall guide us to life everlasting, for His love endures forever.

[46] Matt. 28:20.

Chapter Seven

Christ abides with you
even in times of darkness

∽

"Yea, though I walk in the valley
of the shadow of death,
I will fear no evil,
for Thou art with me."

Besides the paths and dangerous walks in the shepherd
country that would lead the sheep to destruction and
death, there are other paths all encompassed with evils
through which, nevertheless, the sheep are at times
obliged to make their way. There cannot be safety from
all harm for the shepherd's flock. They must in their
journeys encounter many perils, even while pursuing
the proper paths. There are deep and darksome valleys,
walled around on all sides by towering rocky hills, which
at times the shepherd cannot easily escape. And within
these shadowy valleys and somber ravines, there dwell
not infrequently wild and ferocious animals that will, if
aroused, attack and kill the tender sheep. The utmost

care and caution of the shepherd are called into service to conduct his dependent flock safely through these places of deepest peril.

But in spite of all his watchfulness, it sometimes happens that a wolf will get into the very midst of the sheep. The timid, terrified animals become wild with fright and are scattered, running this way and that, until the shepherd calls and bids them gather together. No sooner do they hear his voice, than they all rush swiftly together in a solid mass, and either drive the enemy from their midst or cripple and crush him to death. Thus, in times of greatest peril, the shepherd protects his sheep, and wrests them from the jaws of harm. The sheep know this, and they fear no evils; they know that their master is with them. Although they walk in the shadow of perils and dwell in the midst of the valley of death, they faint not, nor do they fear, for they know that the shepherd is near.

The case of the sheep in the valley of perils is not unlike our own in the midst of the evils of the world; and the peace and safety which we enjoy should also be similar to theirs. We are assured, first of all, by an unflinching faith in God and our Redeemer that, if we trust our Master and obey Him, we shall be led aright throughout our lives, even to the kingdom of Heaven. We shall be led in the paths of justice and love, and crowned at length with the crown of glory, if we but follow the voice of our Shepherd-King and avoid the walks of disaster and ruin. And to hear His voice and to know it, we have but to listen to the teachings of His Church, which will hush to silence our troubled hearts, and direct our wayward feet into the paths of heavenly peace.

Life is full of perils

But, like the shepherd's flock, we not only have to avoid in our journey through life, as perils to our safety and spiritual welfare, the false shepherds and teachers and doctrines that surround us on all sides, but we must also, to pass to our reward, actually encounter inevitable evils and fight many necessary battles. Many of the paths of life through which we must of necessity pass are hard and difficult, and full of deadly perils. We must remember that sin has ruined the primeval beauty of our earthly habitation and made our life here below a labor and a toil to the end.

We not only come into the world with sin on our souls, and are thereby exiles from the city of God, but even when our sin is forgiven us, the remains of the malady continue as wounds in our nature as long as we live on earth. The deadly guilt is wiped away, but the effects of the evil remain. And it is chiefly these wounds of our nature, in ourselves and in others, that render life's journey, even when pursued in accordance with the law of God, at times truly difficult and perilous. Fidelity to God and to His law is not always a safeguard against the wickedness of the world and of men; at times, in fact, it is just the contrary. Indeed, is it not a truth that many, perhaps the majority, of those who endeavor sincerely to please God and to serve Him must often suffer severely for their very goodness and faithfulness? Are they not misunderstood, criticized, and censured? Are they not frequently accused of all manner of wrong, their work disparaged, and their motives impugned? Are not persecution and even martyrdom often their portion?

The worldly imperil your soul

Now, all this is the result of sin. Those who call into question the deeds and motives of God's saints, those who upbraid, and criticize and impute evil to the sincere, faithful servants of God, inflicting upon them dire evils, are but showing the effects of sin in themselves, are but giving exercise to the evil that rules within them. Their particular acts and words may be without present malice; they may be inwardly persuaded that in reviling and condemning their neighbor and doing him harm, they are rendering a service to God Himself. But in so doing, they but manifest the effects of earlier sin — personal, perhaps, and original — which has darkened their understanding and made perverse their moral vision, so that, having eyes, they see not, having ears, they hear not, nor do they understand.[47] Following the corruption of their own nature, bleeding from the wounds of Original Sin, they are prone to blaspheme whatsoever they fail to comprehend;[48] and thus it is that they often make life and the world for the servant of God a truly perilous sojourn, a veritable valley of death.

This failure to be understood, this misjudgment of actions, motives, and deeds — these are doubtless common evils from which, in a measure, we all must suffer. But it is also true that the more elevated the life, the higher its

[47] Matt. 13:13.
[48] Cf. Jude 1:10.

aims, and the loftier the spiritual level on which it pro-
ceeds, the greater the obstacles will be to its being understood and appreciated by the majority, who always tread
the common paths of mediocrity.

A saint is nearly always a disturbance to his immediate surroundings; he is frequently an annoyance and an
irritation to the little circle in which his external life is
cast, simply because he really lives and moves in a sphere
which the ordinary life cannot grasp. Like a brilliant,
dazzling light that obscures the lesser luminaries, and is
therefore odious to them, the man of God is frequently
a disturber of the worldly peace of common men; his life
and works are a living reproach to their lives and works;
and hence, without willing it, he becomes a menace to
their society and is not welcome in their company.

Worldly, plotting minds cannot understand the spiritual and the holy; sinful souls are out of harmony with
the virtuous; the children of darkness cannot find peace
with the children of light. And not only is there a lack of
sympathy in the worldly-minded for the men and women
who are led of God, but there is often positive hatred for
them — a hatred which spends itself in actual, persistent
persecution. To be devout, to refrain from sinful words

and sinful deeds, to shun the vain and dangerous amusements of worldlings, to attend much to prayer and recollection, to love the house and worship of God, to be seen often approaching the sacraments and partaking of the Bread of Life — often, even these holy acts are sufficient to draw down on the servants of God the curse and persecution of a world which knows not what it does.[49]

The worldly persecute the Church

And that which happens individually to the faithful children of God takes place on a larger scale with respect to God's Church. The children of this world, those who have set their heart on temporal things, or who, through willful error, have deviated from the right path to things eternal, never cease from pursuing and persecuting the Church of God. They hate the Church and attack her unceasingly. These ever-living and ever-active enemies of light and truth never abate in their fury against the chosen friends of Christ, and against His holy Church.

But need we be surprised at this? Was it not foretold? Did not our blessed Shepherd, speaking in the beginning

---

[49] Cf. Luke 23:34.

to His little flock, warn them that men would deliver them up in councils and scourge them? Did He not say to them plainly, "And you shall be hated by all men for my Name's sake; but he that shall persevere unto the end, he shall be saved. And when they persecute you in this city, flee into another. . . . The disciple is not above the master, nor the servant above his lord. It is enough for the disciple that he be as his master, and the servant as his lord. If they have called the good man of the house Beelzebub, how much more them of his household."[50]

It happens, therefore, that fidelity to God, and careful adherence to the paths of justice and holiness, can frequently be the occasion of perils and sufferings for us individually, as they also are the excuse for a vaster persecution of the Church in general. All holy persons and holy things are signs of contradiction. They are not of the world; they do not fit in with it; and between them and the world there will be strife and contention until God establishes "the new Heaven and the new earth."[51]

---

[50] Matt. 10:17, 22-25.
[51] Rev. 21:1.

∞

Your sinfulness imperils your soul
But the enemies that lie along the ways of life, that
beset and threaten even the most righteous paths of our
pilgrimage, are not all from without; the most numerous
and menacing are perhaps from within. "The enemies
of a man," says the inspired writer, "are those of his own
household."[52] That is to say, the most potent evils which
we suffer, the chief foes to our present and future
welfare are from ourselves — our own waywardness,
our tendencies to evil, our wilfulness, our self-love and
self-seeking, and our own sins. It is from these and like
causes that we suffer most. Hard and trying it surely is to
bear persecutions and contradictions from others; severe
is the strain to nature when, in the face of our noblest
efforts, proceeding from noblest motives, we meet with
misunderstanding and even condemnation. But to the
upright, religious heart that is sincerely and truly seeking
God amid the shadows and pitfalls of life, the sorest of all
trials and the fiercest of all enemies are one's own temptations and passions and inclinations to evil. It would be

[52] Mic. 7:6; Matt. 10:36.

easier to conquer the whole external world of foes than to reign supreme over the little world within. Of Alexander the Great it is said that, while he actually subdued the whole known world of his time, he nevertheless yielded in defeat before his own passions. He could overcome his external enemies, but surrendered miserably in the battle with self.

Our greatest warfare, then, is the struggle with ourselves, and our greatest victory is the triumph over self. "If each year," says the *Imitation of Christ*, "we could uproot but one evil inclination, how soon we should be perfect men!"[53]

But it is not our lot to be free from enemies and perils, both from without and from within, during our earthly sojourn. They are a part of our lot here below; they are necessarily bound up with the darkened regions through which the Shepherd must lead his flock; and hence, entire safety there shall never be before the journey's end, until we say farewell to present woes, and hail "the happy fields, where joy forever dwells."[54]

---

[53] Thomas à Kempis (c. 1380-1471; ascetic writer), *Imitation of Christ*, Bk. 1, ch. 11.

[54] John Milton, *Paradise Lost*, Bk. 1, line 249.

In our present state, therefore, it is important for us to realize our dangers and to be prepared for conflict. There is no way of escape from crosses, perils, and dreadful battles for all those who wish to win the crown of victory. They must follow the Shepherd as he leads the way, and hence our Lord has said, "If any man will come after me, let him take up his cross daily and follow me."[55] Yes, it is the following of the Shepherd, His leadership, and His constant presence that give comfort to the sheep and dispel the dread and fear of perils. And although we pass through the valley and shadow of death, we need fear no evil, for He is with us.

Suffering can blind you to Christ's presence

At times, frequently perhaps, as we sail the sea of life, the waves roll over and deluge us so completely that we are all but smothered. The clouds gather, thick and black, and overcast the sky of our souls; the sorrows of death surround us, and the pains of the pit encompass us;[56] we are overwhelmed with sadness and plunged in darkness.

[55] Matt. 16:24.
[56] Cf. Ps. 17:5, 6 (RSV = Ps. 18:4, 5).

We think of God, we remember Him, but He seems afar off. The evil which weighs us down — the pain of body, the agony of soul, the sadness and dejection of heart and mind, "the madness that worketh in the brain"[57] — muffle the voice and all but still the trembling pulse, and we are not able so much as to lift our drooping heads and tear-dimmed eyes to see the gentle Shepherd standing faithfully at our side.

It is our failure to discern and apprehend Him that causes extreme agony. If, at these times of utter desolation, when our soul is swept by the winds of sorrow, we could only raise our eyes and thoughts to Him, with faith and hope and childlike trust, the spell would be broken, and we would see the clouds lift and part and float away on the wind, only to let in God's cheerful sun to raise our drooping spirit, and warm and soothe our troubled soul.

But it is difficult, when we are oppressed by sorrow and affliction, to lift our heart and mind to things above. Nature, of itself, tends downward, and unless it has learned to discipline itself and to engage with the enemy in sturdy battle, it is not yet prepared for life. For the world is a

---

[57] Cf. Samuel Taylor Coleridge, "Christabel," Part 2.

battlefield and life a warfare, even from a natural point of view, and only they who have learned to brave the battle, who have prepared themselves for conflict, can hope to win in life's hard contest.

But who is ready for the struggle, and how shall we be able to encounter our foes? Left to ourselves and to our own resources, we shall surely go down in defeat. The opposing forces are too gigantic, too numerous. They throng from near and far. They swarm from within and without, from our own nature and from others, from the world around and from our own household, from those at home and from those abroad. Frequently during life we are, of a certainty, encompassed with perils; we hardly know where to turn or what to do; we are breathless with fright.

But even then, if we have proper faith, we shall grow calm, like the shepherd's flock in the midst of devouring animals and beasts of prey, for our Savior and Shepherd is with us, and no evil can befall us. Even when we think Him farthest away, He is often nearest; when we think Him sleeping, His heart is watching. He loves us, His weak and timid sheep; we are the objects of His heart's affection and ever-active solicitude. If we trust Him, He will not let perish the price of His Precious Blood.

The training we are to receive, and the preparation we are to make, in order to engage worthily and victoriously in the battle of life are nothing, therefore, but lessons of love and trust in the constant goodness and faithfulness of our divine Savior. Unless we viciously drive Him away by deliberate, grievous sin, He is really never absent from us, and least of all when we need Him most. It is our fault if we do not by faith discern Him, if we do not feel His ever-gracious presence. We need to discipline ourselves in acts and deeds of faith and love, and then we shall realize that He is always near us, even in the darkness of the shadow of death.

Strive to know, love, and trust in Christ

We must try to know our Shepherd, first of all; we must endeavor intimately to understand Him. For to have faith in Him, to trust Him, and to believe in His power and goodness, in His overruling care for us and our interests, presuppose a knowledge of Him, just as faith and confidence in an earthly friend follow upon an intimate acquaintance with that friend. But this close knowledge of our Master, so necessary to our present peace and future happiness, will never be ours unless we make Him our confidant, unless we accustom ourselves to live in His presence, to look to Him, to speak to Him often, to listen to His gracious direction. And this intimate relationship with our Savior, this habitual communion with Him, will enkindle in our souls the fire of love.

Once we know Him, we will trust Him, and having faith and confidence in Him, we will link our poor lives to His divine life by the strong cords of heavenly charity. Fear and uncertainty will then be impossible, even in the darkest hours.

It is love, above all, that directs our life — love, indeed, which is born of knowledge. We do not, it is true, love anything before we have some knowledge of it; this would be an impossibility. But once the soul has caught the vision, it is love that drives the life and stimulates and enriches the knowledge.

The objects of our affections are the interpreters of our life and actions. If we love the world, we are led by the world; if we love God, it is God who leads and directs us. "Where the treasure is, there will the heart be also";[58] and where the heart is, there will the life make its way.

[58] Luke 12:34.

But if God is the object of our love, we shall fear no evil, for "God is love," says St. John, "and he who abides in love abides in God, and God abides in Him. . . . There is no fear in love, but perfect love casts out fear, for fear has to do with punishment."[59]

∞

Love of God strengthens you

It is only the love of God, therefore, that will steady our lives, and bear us up in the thick of tribulations. It is the confident assurance that we — although so unworthy — are the objects of divine complacency that awakens in our hearts a return of burning charity, and enables us to say, with the psalmist, when the day is darkest: "The Lord is my light and salvation; whom shall I fear? The Lord is the protector of my life; of whom shall I be afraid?"[60] We are not to fear men, said our Lord, who, when they have destroyed the body, can do no more;[61] neither shall we be in dread of our Master, if armed with the gift of His love, "for fear has to do with punishment," but "love casts out fear."

[59] 1 John 4:16, 18 (RSV).
[60] Ps. 26:1-2 (RSV = Ps. 27:1).
[61] Matt. 10:28.

Rather, mindful of the gift of God, we shall, like the martyrs of old, go bravely forth to the battle of life, or to the slaughter, calmly, hopefully, and cheerfully. While humbly, but steadfastly trustful of the Shepherd who leads us, we shall not be disturbed or troubled; the present shall be shorn of its terrors, the future of its forebodings. This truly is the triumph of life, when love, not fear, has come to rule us. This is the broader, larger life — the forerunner of life eternal in which our days are passed in calm serenity — in which we press on with undaunted tread, under frowning clouds and starlit sky alike; with the joys of friendship around us, or alone amidst the graves of the dead.

We must not infer from this that the love of God, which is our strength, the source of our courage, will blunt our feelings or harden our lives. It does not seal up the fountain of tears, or make us insensible to the pains and sorrows of life, which belong to the lot of all. In a certain sense, it is likely true that those suffer most in life who are most united to God; for they feel most the coldness of the world and its desolation, its want of love and sympathy, its degradation and its misery. Hence it would be a mistake to think that the friends of God in this life are either exempted from pain and sorrow, or made insensible to them, either in themselves or in others. Of these and other evils, they are truly more keenly aware than worldly men, if for no other reason than because of the superior refinement of their nature and the spiritual outlook of their vision.

It is sin, after all, that hardens while it weakens. Sin closes the heart to love. It renders its victims cold, unsympathetic, and selfish, whereas the gifts of grace and holiness are tenderness, mercy, and strength. But although all have to suffer, both the holy and the unholy, the difference between them is this: the ungodly are borne down and overcome by their sorrows and crosses, while the spiritual are always triumphing, even in the midst of apparent defeat. To the foolish, they seem to be vanquished, yet they conquer; often they seem on the verge of surrender, when they emerge in victory; they seem to die, when behold they live![62]

The spiritual man, then, does suffer; he suffers in the cause of God; he suffers for others and for himself. More than this, it is doubtless true that he feels his crosses

[62] Cf. Wisd. 3:2; 2 Cor. 6:9.

more keenly, he grieves more profoundly, than do the children of the world. But through it all he remembers his Savior and is comforted. He knows that the tribulations of the just are many, and that from all these the Lord will soon deliver him,"[63] and he shall not be confounded forever.

[63] Ps. 33:20 (RSV = Ps. 34:19).

Chapter Eight

Christ draws you to Himself through your sufferings

∞

"Thy rod and Thy staff,
they comfort me."

It is already plain to us that the sorrows and sufferings
of the present life are, without doubt, the result and con-
sequence of sin. That we should pass our mortal days so
full of pain and tears, that our fellowman, that the beasts
of the field and the elements, which we need and use as
helpers and servants, and, most of all, that our own nature, with its passions and evil tendencies, should rise
up against us and oppose us, was assuredly not a part of
the original plan.

∞

Sin is the source of suffering
As a wise and all-powerful Designer and Creator,
God founded the world in a masterful fashion — devoid

of evil, free from defect, perfect according to the plans framed in Heaven.

The hills and mountains He founded and set on their bases; the streams and rivers and valleys He formed, all rich and lovely, intended for the comfort and happiness of man; the blue deep He constructed and beautified with its millions of shining wonders. And in all these stupendous creations, in all the diverse works of His mighty, omnipotent hands, there was in the beginning no trace of fault, defect, error, or sin.

The upheaval came when man disobeyed and wrought the commencement of all our woe. And hence it is to man's first disobedience and the fruit of that forbidden tree that we owe all the evils from which our nature suffers and to which our flesh is heir.

But although we know the source of our sorrows and feel the guilt of our sins, this does not make our burden lighter or shorten the path of our pilgrimage. We are confronted by the problem of labor and suffering as soon as we enter the world. No one is entirely exempted, and, strange as it is, we see that it frequently happens that those are most afflicted who are farthest removed from the wickedness of the world and purest in the sight of

God. "Many are the tribulations of the just"[64] — and how true it is that the very fidelity of the servants of God is often an occasion of their sufferings! It is not surprising that sorrow and fear should be the portion of sinners throughout the length of their days, for "destruction and unhappiness are in their ways, and the way of peace they have not known,"[65] but that all, even the saints of God, should suffer alike and be oppressed with miseries is, at first sight, a problem and a baffling mystery.

It is something, indeed, to feel in our suffering that we are paying the debt of our sins, whether personal or original, or both. It is much to know that our crosses, severe and inevitable as they are, are a curb to our wayward nature and a restraint against further sins. It is assuredly a great privilege and a high honor that we, unworthy and unfaithful servants of our Master, should, through our tears and sorrows and sufferings, be enabled to conform our poor lives to the tearful and sorrowful life of our Savior. It is a comfort that words cannot tell to be assured by our faith that amid pains and perils, the Shepherd of our souls is

[64] Ps. 33:20 (RSV = Ps. 34:19).
[65] Ps. 13:3 (this verse does not appear in the RSV).

ever near to shield, to guard, and to save. All of this is surely enough to encourage and strengthen us daily to take up our cross and joyfully follow our Redeemer, even to the hill of Calvary, even to the death of the Cross.

But this is not all. A deeper meaning lies hidden behind the veil of tears, beneath the cloak of pain and sorrow. The miseries of life are not a mere inheritance; neither is their value of a purely negative character. We instinctively feel that somehow, somewhere beyond the scope of mortal ken, there is a higher explanation and a more valid justification for all the failures and pains and sorrows of life than that which appears on the surface of things, or issues in results that are only negative.

Suffering for its own sake was never intended, and we were not made to suffer. We were not created for misery, but for happiness; not for failure, but for victory; not for death, but for life; not for time, but for eternity. And hence, there is a deeper meaning, a higher explanation for all the failures and miseries of the present life than those that are apparent to the casual observer.

The psalmist, referring to the shepherd's care for his sheep, says, "Thy rod and thy staff, they comfort me." The staff the shepherd uses, as already explained, is to assist the sheep along their perilous journeys, and the rod is to protect them from attack. The rod and the staff are necessary for the welfare of the flock, necessary to guide and shield them in their wanderings and to bring them safely home. So, too, it is with us, the children of God. To be properly protected and guided to our happy end, we have need of the rod of affliction and adversity, and likewise of the staff of mercy.

Suffering is not merely punishment for sin

Although human miseries — pain, poverty, suffering, and death — are, as we know, the consequences, just and equitable, of Original Sin, those with short-sighted faith and defective vision find in these crosses only chastisement for sin. Truly, they would never have existed, had we never sinned. But as God, in His mercy, draws good out of evil, so has He made these inevitable results of our transgression serve a higher purpose and minister to noble ends. The Savior came so that we might have life, so that we might progress and advance to ever fuller and more abundant life.[66] His aim, and the aim and purpose

---

[66] John 10:10.

of His heavenly Father, since the very dawn of our creation, has been to lead us to happiness — to perfect, abundant, eternal happiness.

It would be of little account to be happy here unless we are also to rejoice eternally. It would be a poor exchange and a paltry satisfaction, to be present at the feasts of men, only to forfeit our place at the banquet of angels. But our heavenly reward and our celestial crown are to be merited and won here below; they are to follow upon our earthly labors. "Only he shall be crowned," says St. Paul, "who has legitimately engaged in the battle."[67] And did not the Master Himself say, "Let him who wishes to come after me deny himself and take up his cross and follow me"?[68] Did He not declare that we must die in order to live — that we must surrender our life here, if we desire to keep it eternally? "Amen, amen, I say to you, unless the grain of wheat, falling into the ground, dies, it remaineth alone. But if it dies, it bringeth forth much fruit. He that loveth his life shall lose it; and he that hateth his life in this world, keepeth it unto life eternal."[69]

[67] Cf. 2 Tim. 2:5.
[68] Luke 9:23.
[69] Cf. John 12:24-25.

We cannot serve two masters; we cannot serve God and mammon.[70] If we seek to avoid all pain and sorrow, and spend our lives in the pleasures of sense, we must be prepared to forego the future joys of the soul; if we pass our days indulging the flesh and chasing the phantoms of time, we must make ready for the death of the spirit and the forfeit of all that is lasting.

No one can evade life's troubles

We have no choice, then; if we would succeed eternally, we must follow the way of the cross. This is the only way to life — to that abundant, celestial life which our Creator has wished us to live. And it is the bearing of our cross, patiently and resignedly to the will of God, together with our other good works, that enables us to merit, insofar as we can, the joys of the kingdom of Heaven.

But the sufferings and labors, so inevitable and necessary to our earthly state, and which serve as a means to supernal rewards, have still another, deeper meaning, and serve another purpose. We cannot evade them; we must

[70] Matt. 6:24.

encounter them. They are not only unavoidable, but necessary to our dearest interests, as we see, since they are strewn as thorns and brambles all along the narrow way that leads to eternal life. We cannot choose them or lay them aside at will.

We may, indeed, if we are foolish and impious enough, refuse to walk the narrow way of the just and choose the broad road that leads to destruction;[71] but even in that way, we shall not escape the pains and perils inseparable from this mortal life. Or again, we may, in our folly, rebel against the crosses and labors that confront and pursue us; but whether we go this way or that, whether we will it or not, we can no more eschew all the evils of life than escape from the air that we breathe.

The pressure, it is true, is not always upon us; we are not, without ceasing, weighed down by our labors and groaning to be delivered from the body of this death.[72] There is interruption, there is passing pleasure, a rift in the clouds and a smile of the sunshine even for the darkest and poorest life. And yet withal, we know and are

[71] Matt. 7:13.
[72] Cf. Rom. 7:24.

conscious that we are ever under the sentence of death, that life is a fleeting shadow, that like "a flash of the lightning, a break of the wave, man passes from life to his rest in the grave."

There is no evading the conclusion, therefore, that the days of man in this world are few and full of miseries. "The life of man upon earth is a warfare, and his days are like the days of a hireling. He cometh forth like a flower, and is destroyed, and fleeth as a shadow."[73] "For all flesh is as grass, and all the glory thereof as the flower of grass. The grass is withered, and the flower thereof is fallen away."[74]

∞

Suffering can lead you to God

To the natural man, all this is appalling, and how frequently it finds its solution in unbridled self-indulgence, in mental unbalance, and self-destruction! But the saints and all the truly wise have viewed the problem of human suffering in a vastly different light. They have discerned it, first of all, as really distinctive of the road to Heaven,

[73] Job 7:1, 14:2.
[74] Isa. 40:6-7.

and as essentially pertaining to the royal way of the cross. They have understood that it extinguishes the wrath of the heavenly Father, that it atones for sin and makes the soul conformable to our suffering Savior, and therefore have they loved it.

And more than this, those who have been led by the wisdom of God have found not only that the crosses of life are essentially connected with the way of salvation, but that, by them and through them alone, we are often positively driven to God. We may avoid them, and at times, perhaps, succeed; we may flee from them or endeavor to still the voice of their pain; or, when unable to escape them, we may, in our wrath and desperation, rise up against them and rebuke them. But they persistently remain, they continue to haunt, as if to woo and win us to penetrate their deeper meaning, and discover the treasure that in them lies concealed. The very breakdown of human things, the severing of human ties and relationships, the loss of health and wealth, of treasures and friends, and of all that life holds dear, are really meant, in the deepest sense, to drive us to the divine.

This is the meaning of those tears and sorrows, those pains and sufferings, that loneliness, that grief, that agony of heart and soul which belong to this world of tears. All these are intended to teach us that here below, on this crumbling shore of time, we have no abiding city, or home, or life, or love, but we seek a city, a home, a life, a love "that hath foundations, whose builder and maker is God."[75]

We need God. We were made for God, and our nature, with all its longings and powers, cries out for Him. And therefore has God so arranged the world, in spite of all its evils, and in spite of all our sinfulness, that, if we do not prevent it, it will lead us to happiness — lead us to Himself. It was our sin that despoiled the face of the world, but God, in His mercy, has drawn good out of evil. He has made the effects of sin minister to our advantage, if we will but have it so.

We may refuse, because we are free. We may object, and rebel, and oppose our lot. We may take our destiny out of the hands of our Creator and attempt to shape it for ourselves. We may deride and despise the humble, the lowly of heart, the patient, the mortified, and the suffering. We may upbraid the Providence of God and its

[75] Heb. 11:10.

workings, and refuse to submit to the rule of the Creator. We may hold in derision and contempt the little band that is sweetly marching the way of the cross, preferring for ourselves the company of the multitude that does not know God. All this can we do, because we are free.

But if such is our choice, and if we persevere in it, our portion is fixed, and at last we shall have to say with the wicked: "Therefore we have erred from the way of truth, and the light of justice hath not shined unto us, and the sun of understanding hath not risen upon us. We wearied ourselves in the way of iniquity and destruction, and have walked through hard ways, but the way of the Lord we have not known. What hath pride profited us, or what advantage hath the boasting of riches brought us? All those things are passed away like a shadow. . . ."[76]

Sufferings, therefore, are common to all, to the good and the bad, to the wise and the foolish, to the children of light and to the children of darkness. But only those who are directed by grace and light from above are able to pierce the deeper meaning of the cross. All have to bear it, but not all understand it; all feel the weight of it,

[76] Wisd. 5:6-9.

but all do not know the power of it. Like fortune, it knocks at every door; into every heart it endeavors to enter and make known its deeper significance, its hidden secrets, lest any of us should suffer in vain, and our lives be altogether a failure.

To be able to suffer patiently and gladly for God's sake is thus a great wisdom; it is a sign of future blessedness. It is the wisdom of God, which is foolishness to men.[77] "If thou hadst the science of all the astronomers," says Eternal Wisdom, "if thou couldst speak and discourse about God as fully and well as all angels and men; if thou alone were as learned as the whole body of doctors; all this would not bestow on thee so much holiness of life as if, in the afflictions that come upon thee, thou art able to be resigned to me and to abandon thyself to me. The former is common to good and bad, but the latter belongs to my elect alone."

We know that our Savior took upon Himself the Cross of sorrow and suffering, not only so that He might satisfy for our transgressions and be our ransom from bondage, but also so that He might be unto us an example and a

[77] Cf. 1 Cor. 1:21.

leader. And knowing that our unfaithfulness had incurred severe maladies from which none could escape, He bore our infirmities and carried our sorrows for us, in order that we, in our time, might bear our inevitable afflictions for His sake, for love of Him, and thereby attain to unending glory with Him.

∞

Heaven's joys outweigh earth's sufferings

"For the Spirit Himself giveth testimony to our spirit, that we are the sons of God. And if sons, heirs also; heirs, indeed of God, and joint-heirs with Christ: yet so, if we suffer with Him, that we may be also glorified with Him."[78] "If you partake of the sufferings of Christ," says St. Peter, "rejoice that when His glory shall be revealed, you may also be glad with exceeding joy."[79] The chains of sorrow which bind us here below, our Shepherd thus would turn into golden cords of love, which draw and hold us to Him. We cannot, as we see, ascend to Heaven, rise to blessedness, except by the way of the cross.

[78] Rom. 8:16-17.
[79] 1 Pet. 4:13.

And our degree of glory in Heaven, the eternal happiness which we shall enjoy, will be in proportion to the degree of charity, or love of God, which our souls possess at death. And this divine charity, which is to measure our future beatitude, is acquired and augmented by faithfully doing the will of God — by patiently and lovingly bearing the cross of life. Sacrifice is the test of love. And hence the more we do and suffer for Christ's sake, the more we prove our love for Him and the greater shall be our happiness in the kingdom of His Father.

All holy writers, all the masters of the spiritual life, agree in teaching that God particularly chastises those whom He loves with a special love. He tests the elect to find if they are worthy of Himself.[80] He does not spare them now, so that He may spare them hereafter. He tries them for a time, so that He may reward them forever. He seems harsh with them here, during the time of probation, only so that He may draw them closer to Himself everlastingly.

The devoted friends of God and the ardent lovers of things spiritual have deeply pondered these momentous

[80] Cf. Wisd. 3:4, 6.

truths. They have realized that our days here, although few and fast-flying, are really to determine our lot and condition throughout the eternal years. They have known that the passing present is the price of the lasting future; that this is the seeding time, and hereafter the harvest. And because our future happiness is to be in accord with our merits here acquired, jealously have they sought and embraced every present occasion to increase their merits and their worthiness for the glory that is to come.

This is why they have loved the cross, the symbol of salvation, the emblem of victory; this, too, is why they have felt disturbed and full of fear when the cross was absent from them. Unlike the unenlightened sufferer, who sees only punishment in his pains, the saints of God have ever accepted their crosses as a sign of special love, a divine visitation, a preparation for the great communion.

We see now how it is that the rod of chastisement and the staff of mercy are able to give joy and comfort to God's chosen friends; and thus are they designed to console and comfort everyone who is truly led by faith and love. Sufferings are really a blessing, but the eye of faith alone discerns it. They keep us from present pleasures, from hurtful occasions, and from alluring vanities. They direct us into the way of salvation; they drive us to God; they increase the glory of our eternal blessedness.

What are the trials of earth when compared with the joys of Heaven? Rather, how precious are they, since, if we use them aright, they lead us into a higher life, to a closer friendship with God! And if, through the mercy of our heavenly Father, we permit the cross to lead us to Him and enrich our lives with His love, who can speak its infinite value? What treasure can be likened to it? Surely nothing that we know can surpass it in worth.

We might, indeed, enjoy all that life can give; we might possess all riches, all health, and all success. We might have honor, fame, glory, and power, the praise and love of men, the treasures of earthly friendship and earthly affection — the whole world we might gain and enjoy. But if, through all these, or in spite of all, we should not be led to the love and friendship of God, we should know only vanity, and life for us would, in its issue, be nothing but a dismal failure.

But if, on the contrary, through the sufferings and losses, the deficiencies and limitations of life, we have been led to make God our dearest friend, if we have been taught, by the coldness and harshness of men, to take refuge in His love, how blessed are we! How cheaply the purchase has been made, even though it has meant the loss of every passing good, of all that the world can give, even the pouring out of our own life's blood!

Teach me, O my Master,
in the day of sorrow and tribulation,
to understand the meaning of the cross,
to know the value of my sufferings,
and to grasp the power and the secret
of Thy rod and Thy staff.
Assist me to see Thee
through the darkness that surrounds me.
And allow me to feel,
in the midst of loneliness and perils,
amid pain and desolation,
the nearness to my soul of Thy loving kindness,
and the strength of Thy merciful presence.

Chapter Nine

Christ rewards your love for Him

∞

"Thou spreadest
before me a table
in the presence
of mine enemies."

In the preceding verses of the shepherd psalm, the psalmist has described the constant care of the shepherd for his
sheep: the rest and refreshment, the protection and comfort he provides for them. And now he speaks of a feast
he has prepared for them, which is to be likened to a
bountiful banquet — a banquet which they are to enjoy,
a feast which they are to consume, in the sight of their
enemies, in the presence of the evils that afflict them.

He refers, at first, to the manner of preparing, or
spreading, a table in the Orient. Often the custom of
olden times was not much different from that which
prevails among the Arabs even today. To prepare a table
means with them simply to spread a skin or a cloth or a

mat on the ground. And it is to this kind of table that the psalmist refers when he sings of the feast of the sheep. He means nothing more than that he has provided for his flock in the face of their enemies a rich pasture, a spreading slope, where they shall feed with contentment and peace, in spite of the evils that surround them.

Christ's protection brings peace

But the quiet and peace which the sheep enjoy while partaking of their spread-out banquet, are entirely owing to the protecting presence of the shepherd. And it frequently happens that here again the utmost skill and diligence of the shepherd are called into play in thus securing the peace and safety of his flock. The most abundant pastures are many times interspersed with noxious weeds and plants, which, if eaten, would sicken and poison the flock; while around the feeding places and grazing grounds very often lie wild animals, such as jackals, wolves, and panthers, hidden in thickets and holes and caves in the hillsides, ready to spring out at the critical moment and devour the innocent sheep. The shepherd is aware of all these evils and enemies of his tender flock, and he goes ahead and prepares the way, avoiding

the poisonous grasses, and driving away, or slaying, if
need be, the beasts that menace the peace and security
of the pasture. The evils are not entirely dispelled, but
only sufficiently removed or held in check so as not to
imperil the flock.

Such is the table prepared for the sheep by their prov-
ident and watchful shepherd, and such is the feast of
which they partake with quiet joy in the sight and presence of their enemies. But, as was just said, the tranquil
joy which is theirs comes not from the fact that danger
has been all removed, nor from the fact that they have
become hardened and used to its presence. They know it
is always near; and they are conscious, as far as animals
can be, of their own utter helplessness, if left to themselves, to survive an attack from their powerful enemies.
But they do not fear; they are not disturbed or anxious,
solely because that they feel their shepherd is present,
and they know he will guard and protect them. Hence
the psalmist is speaking for the sheep when he says to the
Shepherd with a tone of confident joy: "Thou spreadest
before me a table in the presence of mine enemies."

The spiritual meaning of this, like the other verses of
the shepherd psalm, is peculiarly descriptive of our Lord,

the Good Shepherd of human souls. He, in a manner altogether divine, precedes His elect and prepares the way of salvation for them. He does not deliver them from enemies and dangers, which would be unnatural in the present state, but He makes use of evils, as was said before, to increase the perfection of His chosen souls. Gradually, step by step, He leads them from a natural state to a higher state — from diffidence to trust, from fear to love, from sorrow and anguish to peace and joy.

The change in the soul is rarely at once and immediate; it does not come suddenly. At first, it is difficult and repugnant to nature to find joy in sorrow and pleasure in pain, to see gladness in tears and rest in disturbance, to find peace in the midst of our enemies. But God, in His omnipotent goodness, so disposes and provides for the souls of His elect that sooner or later they penetrate to the meaning of things and find there their hidden treasure.

When the fabric of life itself has crumbled to its native dust, when friends have gone and charms departed, when the very earth we tread seems to tremble beneath our feet and every dream of earthly bliss has fled, when

enemies sit where loved ones sat and the heart has all
but ceased to beat, then is the acceptable time and propi-
tious moment for the devout and faithful soul, which has
washed its garments in the blood of the Lamb, to look
up to Heaven with expectant joy. The thrilling vision of
eternal love so much desired, perhaps so long delayed, is
then, indeed, about to dawn.

The sweetness of God and the peace of His spirit
are not to be found in the marketplace, nor in the noise
and clamor of the busy street. It is not at the banquets
of earthly kings that we taste of the joys of the Savior's
feast. It is not amid honors and riches and the pleasures
of sense that the calm dews of Heaven refresh the soul.
We were made for a higher friendship, for a more intimate union, for a sweeter companionship than any that
earth can provide. And it is only when the door has been
shut to the outer world, when the vanities of time have
ceased to be sought, that the soul is ready for the wedding
garment and able to prepare for the marriage feast. It is
in the inner sanctuary and alone, divested of fleshy trammels and freed from the bondage of earthly attachments
that the soul is able to meet its God and hold intimate
converse with Him.

∽

All are invited to the heavenly banquet

Out of the multitude of souls that are called to the feast which is spread for them, comparatively few ever sit down at the Master's table. Many are invited, and the servant is sent out at the hour of supper to tell them that have been called, that all things are ready, and that they should come. But they tarry; they are not ready; they begin to make excuses and wish to be held excused. Some are entangled in perishable riches and cannot leave their possessions; others are preoccupied with worldly affairs and must not neglect their business; still others are pursuing the pleasures of earth and have no time for the things of Heaven.

But the feast is not for these, after all. The Master invites them; He calls them; He sends His ministers in search of them; He reproves and chides them; He thunders against them to make them hear and obey. But they will not come; they shall never taste of His banquet. He has not spread a table for the proud, the haughty, and the arrogant; He cannot meet in loving communion the worldly, the sensuous, the lovers of ease and hurtful pleasures. Such as these are not prepared to meet Him; they would be out of place and ill at ease in His company; they do not like His society.[81]

To be able to come to the Master and to sit at His feast, there is need of preparation. The garments of the world must be changed for the garments of Heaven; the ways of men must be made to yield to the ways of God. For what is wisdom with men is foolishness with God;[82] the weak things of earth are the strong things of Heaven; the outcast of the world are the chosen of the Father Almighty. And hence, our Savior, under the figure of the master in the parable who prepared a great supper, says of all those who will not hear Him, who neglect His divine inspirations and despise the call of His ministers, that they shall never taste of His feast.

∞

Those who embrace the cross enter Heaven

But who, then, shall sit down at His table? For whom has He prepared the banquet? He tells us Himself: those who shall partake of His supper are the lowly, the humble, the poor, the lame, and the blind; the despised of

---

[81] Luke 14:16-24.
[82] 1 Cor. 1:25.

men and the outcast of the people; those who have known sorrow and suffering and penance, who have found the way of the cross and embraced it, who, for the kingdom of Heaven and the love of Christ crucified, have given up father and mother and wife and children and brothers and sisters, yes, and their own life also, that they might inherit everlasting crowns that do not fade away.[83]

St. Paul was one of these masterful spirits, who surrendered all that he had, all that he prized most dearly for love of Christ and His service. "The things that were gain to me," he says, "the same have I counted as loss for Christ. Furthermore, I count all things to be but loss for the excellent knowledge of Jesus Christ my Lord, for whom I have suffered the loss of all things, and count them as waste, that I may gain Christ."[84]

What a struggle, too, was that which St. Augustine describes, speaking of his own conversion! The parting with those sinful delights which had hitherto held him in chains was like the forfeiture of all he possessed, and it seemed to him that life thereafter would not be worth

[83] Cf. Luke 14:26.
[84] Cf. Phil. 3:7-8.

living; yet he generously and vigorously gave them up
so that Christ might become his possession. He has also
described for us the change. "How sweet," he says, "did
it at once become to me to want the sweetness of those
trifles, which to lose had been my fear, but which to have
lost was now a joy! Thou didst cast them forth from me,
O Thou true and highest sweetness! Thou didst cast
them forth and, in their stead, didst enter in Thyself,
sweeter than all pleasure!"[85]

It is such as these heroic souls, who, for the sake of
God and His kingdom, have made the world their enemy,
that compose the company of the elect. And for these
alone, the Shepherd of souls has spread a table of rest and
peace, even in this life, of which they partake in the sight
of their enemies, in the presence of those who think evil
of them, who despise and deride them, in the sight of the
world which hates them. These holy souls, the elect of
God, whom the Father has chosen for Himself have
learned, through the trials and losses of life, the lessons
of peace and detachment which crosses are intended to
teach. They have learned, by exclusion and retirement

[85] St. Augustine (354-430; Bishop of Hippo), *Confessions*,
Bk. 9, ch. 1.

from worldly festivities and pernicious delights, to draw near to God, out of love for His beauty and mercy, or if only to ease their breaking hearts and dispel the loneliness of their forsaken lives. In the words of the psalmist, they have tasted and seen that the Lord is sweet, and that there is no one like unto God.[86]

With the image of the Crucified before their eyes and conscious of the presence of their loving Shepherd, they greet with delight the sufferings that oppress them, and they feast in peace in the presence of their enemies. They know that all is arranged or permitted by the hand that guards them, and by the One who loves them. And, "although He slay them, yet will they trust Him."[87] For what can happen to those who love God? What evil can befall them? Angels have charge over them to keep them in all their ways.[88]

It is confidence, therefore, in their Savior and God that gives peace and tranquillity to the souls of the just. To know Him, to love Him, to trust Him, to dwell in His presence, and to please Him, throughout all the

[86] Ps. 33:9, 112:5 (RSV = Ps. 34:8, 113:5).
[87] Cf. Job 13:15.
[88] Cf. Ps. 90:11 (RSV = Ps. 91:11).

vicissitudes and evils of life, are the objects of their con-stant actions and the highest aspirations of their fervid souls. Confident of the favor and protection of God, and rooted in His love, they do not fear pain and the threats of men; and in the midst of the battle of life, they rejoice in a peace of mind and soul of which the worldling cannot dream. The pasture in which they feed, and the banquet of which they partake are nothing other than the love and friendship of God, which nourishes and refreshes their spirits, when, to every mortal eye, they seem desti-tute, abandoned, and alone.

And this "peace of God, which surpasseth all under-standing,"[89] develops in truly spiritual souls a habit of mind and a character of life that even here below partake of the stability and calm sense of victory which, in their perfection, belong only to the state of the blessed in Heaven. They feel that "all things are possible to them through Him that strengtheneth them,"[90] and that no temporal affliction, no power of man or any creature shall wrest from them the feast which they enjoy.

[89] Phil. 4:7.
[90] Cf. Phil. 4:13.

And hence they are able to ask, in the confident words of the Apostle, "Who shall separate us from the love of Christ? Shall tribulation, or distress, or famine, or nakedness, or danger, or persecution, or the sword? . . . In all these things, we overcome, because of Him that hath loved us. Therefore we are sure that neither death, nor life, nor angels, nor principalities, nor powers, nor things present, nor things to come, nor might, nor height, nor depth, nor any other creature, shall be able to separate us from the love of God, which is in Christ Jesus, our Lord."[91]

[91] Rom. 8:33-39.

Chapter Ten

Christ diminishes
the fear of death

∞

"Thou anointest
my head with oil;
my cup runneth over."

"Thou anointest my head with oil; my cup runneth over": in these words, the psalmist alludes to one of the most touching offices performed by the good shepherd toward his sheep. The day is drawing to a close, the golden orb of light has sunk to rest, and the shadows are creeping up the hills. The hush of night is falling around, and the shepherd must gather his flock into the fold. The labors, the journeys, the trials, the wanderings of the day are over, and now comes the time for rest. It is a scene full of peace, and the sheep greet its approach with feelings of restful anticipation. Many of them are foot-sore and lame; many have received bruises and scratches during the journeyings of the day; some have gaping and bleeding wounds from the attacks of wild beasts; others are simply tired out and exhausted from the long walks and climbing of steep hills.

The shepherd knows all this, and before leading the sheep to rest, he takes care to see that the wounds of all are dressed and soothed, so that nothing shall disturb the sweet repose of their sleep. For this purpose, he stands at the door of the fold as the sheep pass in. He has olive oil and cedar tar to use as healing ointments for their wounds, and he has cool, refreshing water for those that are worn and weary. Lovingly and tenderly he regards each member, as one by one they enter into rest; and they that are wounded or over-weary he holds back with his rod, until their scars and sores are duly cared for and made ready for the night's repose.

How closely these offices performed for the sheep by the shepherd resemble the care of our Father and Savior providing at the end for the souls that He loves! He has been with them all through life, leading, guiding, guarding, and shepherding them at all times, going before them with the blessings of goodness. And when at length the end approaches, these souls feel the need of His loving kindness perhaps more than ever before.

∞

Christ meets the spiritual needs of all

Like the shepherd's flock, their needs are many and various. There are some souls who, through the special grace of God, are able to pass their lives in innocence and holiness, living in the world, yet not *of* it, dwelling in the midst of men and in the sight of their wickedness and sin, yet undefiled withal, beautiful witnesses of the power and love of Him who strengthens and preserves them.

But the majority are not thus favored. Notwithstanding all their graces, they have been subject to falls — perhaps to many grievous falls. They have suffered many wounds and bruises. They have had many tears to shed. Multitudes there are, in fact, who come down to the verge of life, to the very gate of death, sin-stained, racked and wounded, their lifeblood ebbing out through sores and wounds which they themselves have made by willful open friendship with sin and vice, the deadly foes of their souls. We have many varying examples of these straying souls.

Consider Mary Magdalene, St. Peter, St. Paul, and St. Augustine. They passed a portion, brief or prolonged, of their mortal days far from the Father's home, feeding on the husks of swine, but who, while yet in the vigor of life, felt the touch of the merciful hand and heard the sound of the loving voice, leading them, calling them back to God, back to the "beauty ever ancient and ever new."[92]

Such souls as these, it is true, constitute one class of erring, but repenting sinners, but there is another class whose plight is far more pitiable. They are those long-delayed, but finally repentant sinners, men and women who have lived their lives away from the Church and her sacraments, who have grown old and gray in the sins of their youth, and now, at last, when death is coming, are moved, by a special grace from Heaven, to weep for their sins and wasted years before they enter their eternal abode.

For each and all of these, how important it is that the Shepherd should stand at the door of the fold and bind up their wounds with His tender grace before they pass through death's portals! Scarred and wayward children, victims of evil circumstances, creatures of vanity and folly, they realize at the end how impotent they are, how helpless they are in the presence of the coldness of death to

[92] St. Augustine, *Confessions*, Bk. 10, ch. 27.

redeem the years that have fled, unless He who has sustained them in life, and who is at once the Author and Master of both life and death, draws near and assists them!

But for all, without exception, the need of the Shepherd is imperative at the end. The victory, the happy issue of life's struggle, "is not of him that willeth, nor of him that runneth, but of God that sheweth mercy."[93] All may run, all may strive, indeed, for the prize of eternal life, but none can be sure, short of the mercy of God, that he will be saved; none can merit this crowning glory of life. Whether young or old, whether favored or neglected, whether innocent or guilty, whether the life has been dowered with special blessings and never known the stain of grievous sin, or whether it has been eked out amid deepest misery and defiled with hateful crimes, the same uncertainty as to the manner in which the end shall come remains for all.

∽

Perseverance is a gift from God

Men may reason and conjecture, from what they see and know, that this one or that one is in God's favor, and

---

[93] Rom. 9:16.

shall so persevere to the end. They may reason that the members of a certain family, or class, or station in life are sure to be saved, and shall never fall short, but that those of another class or condition shall, on the contrary, die as they have lived, in the filth of their sins, to be forever in torment. But these are the reasonings of men, which are of no avail in the sight of God. It is only the Father in Heaven who knows the elect. He alone is able to tell who shall remain to be crowned, and who is to be condemned.

Perseverance is a gratuitous gift of God; we cannot merit it. All our good actions and holy deeds, which are performed in the state of grace and out of a motive of charity, do, it is true, merit a reward in Heaven; they tend to increase our blessedness hereafter. But just as it is not in our power to merit the first grace, by which we are raised from a state of sin, so are we utterly unable to do anything which shall secure for a certainty the final grace, by which alone we can be saved. Wherefore the preacher said, "All these things have I considered in my heart, that I might carefully understand them: there are just men and wise men, and their works are in the hand of God; and yet man knoweth not whether he be worthy of love or hatred. But all things are kept uncertain for the time to come, because all things equally happen to the just and to the wicked, to the good and to the evil, to the clean and to the unclean, to him that offereth victims, and to him that despiseth sacrifices. As the good is, so also is the sinner; as the perjured, so he also that sweareth truth."[94]

This uncertainty as to the end of life, and of the gift of final perseverance, all holy souls have felt. To die in the friendship of God, and thence to enjoy His presence forever, is a gift of so transcendent a nature, so far above our natural powers and utmost deserts that no creature which can at all conceive it would dare claim it as a right.

It was this conviction that made the saints tremble to think of it. It was this that prompted St. Paul to admonish the Philippians to work out their salvation "with fear and trembling,"[95] and that also evoked from the same apostle those candid words concerning himself: "I chastise my body, and bring it into subjection, lest, perhaps, when I have preached to others, I myself should become a castaway."[96]

[94] Eccles. 9:1-2.
[95] Phil. 2:12.
[96] 1 Cor. 9:27.

And have we not sometimes witnessed instances which, so far as man can judge, give ground for this fear as to perseverance, and emphasize the great truth that to die in God's favor is, indeed, a singular and a gratuitous gift?

How many have we known who started well, but terminated ill! How many are innocent and holy in youth and give every promise of splendid manhood, but fade and drop, like poisoned flowers, before the age of maturity has dawned! How many are able to pass through the most critical period of their lives, unshaken and undefiled, full of faith, hope, love, and purity, but who, when the age of security is thought to have come, lose the grip which seemed so firm, turn to evil, yield to vicious habits, and die reprobates of God!

Look at King Solomon. Who was ever more promising than he in his youth? Whoever gave fairer prospects of continued holiness and of a beautiful end? He was so lovely, so amiable, so favored of God in the morning of life; graced with such high perfections, not knowing evil, a stranger to vice, a lover of sanctity, of wisdom, and of grace. It would seem that he could never fall — he who was the object of such unwonted favors, who dwelt so supremely in the smile of Heaven. But behold the end of him who had received so many graces, who chose wisdom as his handmaid so that he might be guided aright. Behold that youthful figure, so full of promise and goodly hope, praying to God that he might never deviate from the ways of grace. And then see the gray-haired apostate tottering to the grave, borne down by the weight of his sins and of his years.

And how many more there have been, such as King Saul, such as Voltaire[97] and numerous others whom we ourselves perhaps have known, who were great and good in youth, and for a term of years, but whose end was a miserable failure!

Our perseverance, then, or the favor to die in the state of grace, is not of ourselves, not the reward of our efforts, or of our good works, "but of God who sheweth mercy." We must do all in our power to merit eternal life; we must press on toward the mark, waging ceaseless battle in behalf of God and of our souls, even to the last moment. But for the happy end of it all, we must perforce rely on the tender mercy of God. This is why our Lord, before He

[97] François-Marie Arouet Voltaire (1694-1778), French writer and philosopher.

departed from earth, prayed to His heavenly Father
for His disciples: "Holy Father, keep them in Thy Name,
whom Thou hast given me. . . . I pray not that Thou
shouldst take them out of the world, but that Thou
shouldst keep them from evil."[98] This truth the psalmist
also had in mind when he prayed: "Perfect Thou my
goings in Thy paths, that my footsteps be not moved."[99]

∞

Uncertainty causes fear of death

It is this appalling uncertainty about the end and
outcome of life, together with our own inability to make
them secure, that makes death so terrible to the minds
and thoughts of multitudes, even of Christians and
well-living persons. They fear to fall into the hands of
the living God. For them, the present life may be not
so attractive — on the contrary, it is most likely replete
with pain and toil; but somehow they wish to linger here,
preferring that which is certain, although so miserable, to
that which is doubtful, perhaps awful and irreparable. So
long as they continue in this present world, there is

[98] John 17:11, 15.
[99] Ps. 16:5 (RSV = Ps. 17:5).

chance for change; there is hope of improvement. But when death intervenes, and the soul is removed to the other life, all hopes of change are swept away, and the lot of the soul is fixed for eternity.

There is, of course, a fear of death which is altogether natural. Many who pretend not to believe in a future life, or even in the existence of God, dread death. And many there are whose lives are holy, and who have no reason to fear, but for whom, nevertheless, the very thought of death is fraught with all manner of terrors. As some are naturally afraid in the absence of light, and tremble with fear at being alone in a dark and lonely place, so there are many who, without assignable reason, other than a native tendency, are appalled at the thought of death.

But when all due allowances have been made for the uncertainty of final perseverance, and for the anxiety arising from natural temperament, it seems not too much to say that, for the most part, the fear and dread of death which haunts so many Christians can be reduced to two causes: a defect of faith or a love of the world. It is one of these causes, or both of them together, which alone can explain, in the majority of cases, why such numbers of Christians and Catholics are unwilling to surrender the present life, and are disturbed at the very thought of dying. Either they do not realize by faith the surpassing glories of the life beyond — doubting its reality, questioning its nature, misunderstanding the goodness and mercy of God; or else they are so attached to the present existence that all serious thought and desire for a better life are excluded from their minds and hearts.

Fénelon[100] says that the condition of our spiritual life is indicated by the answers we give to the following questions: "Do I love to think of God? Am I willing to suffer for God? Does my desire to be with Him destroy my fear of death?" We do not fear to meet or to be with one whom we really love, for "love casts out fear." There is no dread at the coming of the parent or friend whom we truly love, unless, perchance, we have offended him, and lack full faith that we have been forgiven and reinstated in his favor and friendship.

∞

Lack of trust causes fear of death

So it is with God. If we are unwilling to meet Him, or filled with fear at the approach of His coming, it seems

---

[100]François Fénelon (1651-1715), Archbishop of Cambrai.

certain that our faith is at fault. Why should we not wish to meet Him who has made us, who loves us, who has washed away our sins with His own blood, who alone can comfort our trembling souls and fill us with every good? Perhaps we have sinned and betrayed our Maker many times and grievously in our lives, and the voices of those sins are haunting us, and bidding us beware of the hour of death and of the judgment that follows. Perhaps there is a lurking suspicion that we have not been forgiven, a temptation that we are not sincere, a feeling that our sins are too grave to be pardoned, a conviction that we do not belong to the company of the elect.

We may have notions, moreover, altogether severe, of the nature of God and of His justice. We feel His immensity and sanctity, we have heard so much of His ineffable beauty, that, weighed down with a sense of our nothingness, of our poverty and misery and sinfulness, we cannot but shudder at the thought of appearing in His presence. These and similar terrors may take hold of us and fill us with a dread of death.

But is it not clear that, whatever their cause, these fears are born of a lack of faith? We do not trust, as we ought, the Shepherd who loves us; we are not convinced of His mercy and kindness if we do not believe with childlike confidence that He stands ready ever to forgive and bless the least of His children who humbly and sincerely seek Him, asking for the help they need.

The severity of God toward sinners endures only so long as they refuse to acknowledge their guilt. His harshness with them, like that of Joseph with his brethren,[101] is but love in disguise; and as soon as they are brought to own their guilt, that which before was the anger of God is swiftly turned into His love and mercy.

Christ did not come to destroy, but to save. He will not "crush the broken reed, nor extinguish the smoking flax."[102] "As a father hath compassion on his children, so hath the Lord compassion on them that fear Him, for He knoweth our frame; He remembereth that we are dust."[103]

∾

Love of the world causes fear of death

But there is also the love of the world, which enslaves so many. So numerous and so bewitching are the attractions of the present life that some men are loath to leave

[101]Gen. 42-45.
[102]Cf. Isa. 42:3.
[103]Ps. 102:13-14 (RSV = Ps. 103:13-14).

them. It is a beautiful world, this universe of ours —
so deep, so wide, so vast! It is filled with pleasures and
allurements and graced with myriad charms. And he
who can easily turn from its enchanting beauties and
close his ear to its manifold voices seems cold of heart
indeed.

Ponder for a moment the richness of nature, its similarity and variety, its sameness and its diversity. Consider
the abundance of the harvest: the glowing fruits, the
green and golden crops, the sweet-scented flowers, and
gift-bearing grasses. See the stars above and the waters
beneath — all the wonders of earth and sky.

And then, when you have ranged over fields and
waves and mountains, when you have climbed up the
steps of the sky and gazed on the marvels of the heavens,
descend again to earth and consider the human form —
the chief work of the almighty hand, and the crown of
the natural world. What beauties are here concealed!
What a mingling of material and spiritual, of human and
almost divine! What words can express, what lines can
portray the beauty of the human countenance? Who can
describe or adequately define the loveliness that streams
from human eyes, or echoes from the human voice? And

yet these are but the outer fringes and dimmest glimpses of the beauties of the soul that dwells within.

How painful, then, it is for the worldly to forsake the beauties and pleasures of this present life. Bound to their beds of clay by the things of sense, they are grieved to part with a life so full of diverse attractions. How can they think undismayed of closing forever their eyes and ears to these charms of color and sound? It is such a difficult thing, and so hard for nature, to abandon these scenes of enticing pleasure, to bid farewell to those who are dear and be hurried away alone and forlorn to the chill and gloom of the grave.

So reason the children of the world, but are not their reasonings and feelings a proof of their little faith, and of their poor conceptions of spiritual and eternal interests? They do not want to leave the world, because they love it; and they love the world because their faith is too weak to raise them to a vision of higher things. The plain on which they stand is too low to see the things of Heaven clearly.

∞

Those with faith do not fear death

How poor and trifling, at best, is the earth and all it contains to him who beholds with a vivid faith the world above that is to come! How gladly does he lay down his life and turn away from its ceaseless battles, who sees by faith, just beyond the portals of death, the great home of the blessed, spread out like a city on the mountains, bathed in light inaccessible, full of joy and unending gladness, where "death shall be no more, nor mourning, nor crying, nor sorrow shall be anymore."[104]

The man of faith, therefore, is in no way straitened or disturbed by the approach of death. He has learned to know and to trust the good Master whom he serves. Like the apostle Paul, he is concerned only that Christ should be glorified in him at all times and in all things, "whether it be by life or by death," for to him also, "to live is Christ, and to die is gain."[105] He lives in the world, but is not *of* it; he treads the ways of earth, but he really belongs to the kingdom above.

Hence his cup of interior peace is ever running over. Although surrounded by many evils, he does not faint; although tempted exceedingly, he does not yield, but is joyous and peaceful withal, because at all times and in all

[104]Rev. 21:4.
[105]Phil. 1:20-21.

things he feels himself to be the faithful servant of God, "in much patience, in tribulation, in necessities, in distresses, in strifes, in prisons, in seditions, in labors, in watchings, in fastings, in chastity, in knowledge, in long-suffering, in sweetness, in the Holy Spirit, in charity unfeigned . . . as dying, and yet living; as chastised, and not killed; as sorrowful, yet always rejoicing; as needy, yet enriching many; as having nothing, yet possessing all things."[106]

Christ brings sweetness even to death

"Precious in the sight of God is the death of His saints."[107] As they have lived for Christ, they gladly welcome the summons that calls them home to rest. Calmly and fearlessly they go down to death; joyously and with feelings of exultation they hail the coming of Him on whom their thoughts have rested throughout life, of Him whom they have ever seen by faith, whom they have loved, whom they have trusted, whom they have chosen for their own. Confident of the power and goodness of

[106]Cf. 2 Cor. 6:4-10.
[107]Ps. 115:15 (RSV = Ps. 116:15).

their faithful Shepherd, pain daunts them not, the enemy worries them not. The last hour for them is not one of darkness, but of light; it is a time not for lamentations, but for joyous and gladsome strains.

The end may be sudden, or it may be gradual in its approach; it may come early, or late in life; it may be at home or abroad; it may be in the winter, or it may be in summer, on the sea or on the land. But to the just and spiritual, it can never be a surprise; it can never be lonely, never sad. It is the time for which they have always longed — a time of liberation, of emancipation from the trammels of earth and flesh, the end of continuous dying and the beginning of lasting life.

What a supreme moment, what a joyous event is death for a just and holy soul! What sweet emotions must thrill the spirit, as the Savior stoops over the bed of death to wipe away forever the last of earthly tears! Mary is there to hush the voice of reproach and to whisper words of peace, Jesus has come to claim the soul and take it to Himself, and flights of angels are waiting to sing it to its rest.

Chapter Eleven

Christ calls you to trust in Him

∞

"Surely goodness and mercy shall follow me
all the days of my life; and I shall dwell
in the house of the Lord
unto length of days."

If the tender lambs and timid sheep of the shepherd's
flock could speak the sentiments of their innocent hearts,
each one would certainly voice the words which here
the psalmist has uttered for them all: "Surely goodness
and mercy shall follow me all the days of my life; and
I shall dwell in the house of the Lord unto length of
days."

Throughout the live-long day, throughout all the
days of their lives, they experience the shepherd's goodness; they are the objects of his constant mercy. He has
been caring for them since their birth; he has led them
out each morning since they were first able to walk; he
has provided them with food, and led them to water; and

he has ever been present to shield them from harm and to protect them from their enemies.

After such repeated experiences and trials of his loving kindness, they have grown accustomed to his faithfulness and are filled with love of his goodness and mercy. And while they have not the power of speech, and cannot by words express their feelings, they do so by the louder voice of action — by their quiet trust in his care, by their habitual mildness and gentleness and quick response to his every word, by the absence of solicitude and fear in view of his presence. By these and all the other actions that reveal what is in their simple hearts, they show their love for their shepherd.

Although often wounded and bleeding and exhausted from the roughness and length of their journeys, they have no distrust about the future, no fear for the morrow. In the midst of distress, the shepherd, they know, will provide.

The psalmist, therefore, in the closing words of the shepherd psalm, gives utterance to the feelings of the sheep when he sings, "Surely goodness and mercy shall follow me all the days of my life, and I shall dwell in the house of the Lord unto length of days."

∞

See the signs of God's abiding help

But here, as in the opening verse of the shepherd psalm, the words of the sacred psalmist, although truly expressive of the sentiments of the sheep, are more directly the expression of his own inner feelings, and of the feelings of all faithful souls toward the Lord who rules and guides them. All those whose lives have been really and sincerely led by faith, have, like the shepherd's flock, grown trustfully accustomed, in the course of years, to the goodness and mercy, to the faithfulness and love of the hand that provides for them.

As they look into their lives, and retrace the steps they have taken, they cannot fail to see how God has been always with them, patiently enduring their faults, mercifully binding up their wounds and hurts, and lovingly leading, drawing them to Himself. They can see their advancement, as slow, perhaps, as it has been, and they know it is God who has given the increase.[108]

Looking now at their lives through the perspective of the years that are gone, how many problems they have

[108] 1 Cor. 3:6.

been able to solve! For how many apparent mysteries they have found an explanation! All those crosses and trials, all those struggles and battles with the enemy, all those attacks from within and assaults from without, all, in fact, that they have ever endured — their sins alone excepted — they now can trace, through the light of faith, back to the hand of their Father in Heaven.

Not everything, indeed, has yet been explained, but enough, indeed, is sufficiently clear to remove every doubt from the faithful soul as to the goodness and Providence of God. And hence the soul exclaims with the psalmist, out of the abundance of its faith and confidence, "Surely goodness and mercy shall follow me all the days of my life; and I shall dwell in the house of the Lord unto length of days."

∞

Spiritual fruitfulness calls for trust in God

It is doubtless a lack of implicit trust in God and Divine Providence which, more than anything else, accounts for the unhappiness and spiritual barrenness of so many Christian and religious lives. Poor and scanty is the fruit they yield, simply because they have no depth of soil; they are not deeply and firmly rooted in faith and confidence in God.[109] Like reeds shaken by the wind, like houses built on the sand, they tremble and shake with every blast, they are all but overturned by every tempest that rises.[110]

And it is not surprising that this should be so. The higher gifts of the spirit come from God, and hence the good fruit which the spirit yields is also traceable back to Him. "We do not gather grapes from thorns, nor figs from thistles; and as a good tree cannot bring forth evil fruit, so neither can an evil tree bring forth good fruit."[111] And just because the abundance of the harvest of the spiritual life is dependent upon God as its giver, is it strange that any distrust of Him and His Providence should be a great hindrance to the soul's advancement, and to the bestowal of the constant help it needs? Can God be pleased with those who do not confide in Him, and who do not trust Him?

Our Lord's own chiding words to His disciples are a proof of His displeasure at any distrust in His power and goodness. How often did He rebuke them for their want

[109]Cf. Matt. 13:5-6.
[110]Cf. Matt. 11:7, 7:26-27.
[111]Cf. Matt. 7:16-18.

of confidence in Him? How often did He accuse them reproachfully of their "little faith,"[112] of being "slow of heart,"[113] of being an "unbelieving and perverse generation"?[114] He was constantly pointing to their lack of faith, reminding them that it was the source of their weakness, the cause of their ignorance in things spiritual, and the reason for their powerlessness in the face of difficulties and against the enemies of their souls. It is clear that Almighty God, being a generous and loving Father, must be offended at those of His children who do not trust Him; and their want of faith in Him is consequently the reason they do not receive the help which is the life of their souls, and without which they are powerless to be useful servants in His vineyard.

And this failure to confide in the goodness of God betrays itself in other ways. Besides sealing up the fountains of special graces and closing the door on divine generosity, besides a general unfruitfulness in the spiritual life, and the lack of all greater works for God and for souls, which are its immediate consequences, it also penetrates

[112]Matt. 6:30.
[113]Luke 24:25.
[114]Matt. 17:16.

into the interior sanctuary of the spirit, and weakens at their source the springs of spiritual action. The results are manifest. Not only is there no yielding of fruit, but growth is likewise wanting. And if, under fairer conditions, there has ever been any progress, it is soon perceived to wither and wane in a soul devoid of living faith.

All the exercises and practices of the Christian life participate in the baneful effects. Prayer and the use of the sacraments are either seriously neglected or gradually given up, and the blighting influences of irreligion rapidly spread and overrun all areas of life. The view one takes of God, and the faith — or lack of faith — and trust one has in Providence have their effect on the character and give a direction to all one's ways of thinking, feeling, and acting, in regard to the world we live in, in regard to mankind in general, and in regard to the causes, purposes, and destinies of all things.

Our conceptions of Providence are vital therefore. They really determine what our life is to be, and they are an index to the life that is finished. It is impossible that we should be quite the same whether we try to eliminate God from our lives, or allow His blessed influence to cheer and lead us; whether we look upon Him as a cold

Master, waiting to exact and punish, or as a kind Father and Shepherd, seeking to spare and save; whether we regard Him as hidden far in the heavens, caring naught for the creatures and the world He has made, or whether we conceive Him as intimately bound up with all the works of His hands, although distinct from them, as guiding and regulating everything, as tenderly loving and providing for all the needs of our souls.

Trust in God above all

Another most harmful result of deficient faith and confidence in God is that it leads us to trust in creatures. It causes us to reverse the proper order of things. We are dependent beings, and we instinctively feel our deficiencies and the need of someone or something on which to lean, at times, and to which we can look for assistance. We may not be entirely and always conscious of this tendency in us, we may be too proud or too blind to admit it, or we may wish we could overcome it and rid our lives of so constant a need. But whether we see it and acknowledge it or not, whether we encourage it or try to repress it, the need is always there, deeply engraved in our nature as creatures, and we cannot help but seek to satisfy it.

There is not one of us, frail beings that we are, who is entirely sufficient unto himself.

Sometimes, of course, the voice of our needs is silent, and we feel that we shall never want. "I said in my abundance," observes the psalmist, "I shall not be moved forever."[115] But when the tide begins to ebb and prosperity subsides, how soon do we remember that we are dust! How frequently, in times of trouble, in times of illness and poverty and suffering when face-to-face with our foes, or when death steps in and slaughters, are we made aware of our insufficiency, and of our utter helplessness to live our lives alone and meet single-handed the burdens and misfortunes of earth! It takes but a little frost to nip the root of all our greatness, and then when our high-blown pride breaks under us, we quickly realize how fragile and insecure are the personal foundations of our lives. Naturally and reasonably, therefore, did the pagan philosophers conclude that friendship and friends were necessary to man.

Profoundly aware of this fundamental need of help and support, which is a result of our nature, we habitually

[115]Ps. 29:7 (RSV = Ps. 30:6).

stretch out our hands to others, not only during the years of infancy and childhood, but to a greater or lesser extent throughout the whole period of our earthly existence. At first, of course, it is to creatures that we necessarily look — to parents, relatives, guardians, teachers, and later on, to friends and acquaintances. Our needs in the beginning and in early years, although many and imperative, are comparatively simple; they can be satisfied by those around us. But as we advance to maturity and take in more completely the meaning of our lives, and consider not so much the needs of the body as the demands of the soul, we find that the multiple requirements of infancy and youth, which were able to be supplied by those who were near, have given way to the fewer, but vast and unlimited claims of age, which express the wants of the spirit.

It is when we appeal to creatures for the complete and permanent satisfaction of these latter necessities of our being that we seriously err, and open the way to disappointment and sorrow. This is not to say that we are to have no cherished and chosen friends, or that we should despise the needs and gifts, the privileges and blessings of friendship, which, in truth, our nature requires; nor again that we are to regard with skeptical, disdainful eyes the world and human nature; but we must not deceive ourselves by trying to find in any created being that which it does not possess. We must not endeavor to get from any creature that perfect satisfaction which we need and which the Creator alone can give. Neither must we seek to fill the unlimited capacity of our souls with only those gifts, poor and defective at best, which frail mortals like ourselves are able to supply. It is folly in the highest degree to expect from anyone less than God that which only God can afford.

The mistake, therefore, is made when creatures of any kind are allowed to take the place of God, when they are sought and reposed in as an end in themselves, and as sufficient satisfaction for the needs of the human spirit. Unwise, indeed, is this mode of action, and bitter are the sorrows of soul to which it inevitably leads!

One man trusts in riches, another in glory, another in the esteem of men; one leans upon his friends and companions, another upon his relatives — all forgetful of the frail and unsubstantial nature of every earthly prop. Frequently they never awaken to the peril of their state until they find themselves face-to-face with their doom and the awful disillusionment.

The crash may be delayed, but the day must come sooner or later for all of us who have advanced but a little beyond maturity, when all the natural lights of life go out, when every human prop is removed, and we find ourselves out alone and in the dark, unable to receive any more assistance from the world and creatures. How miserable then shall we be if we have put our trust in men, if we have tried to make creatures play the part in our lives which only God can play! When we need them most, they fail us, when we fain would find beneath their protection a shield against the fiery darts of life, behold they wither like the ivy of Jonah[116] and leave us alone in our want!

How vain, therefore, and groundless is that confidence which is put in men, and how wretched that poor man who hangs on princes' favors! "Thou trusteth in money," says St. Augustine, "thou holdest to vanity; thou trusteth in honor; and in some eminence of human power, thou holdest to vanity; thou trusteth in some principal friend, thou holdest to vanity. When thou trusteth in all these things, either thou diest and leavest them

---

[116]Jon. 4:6-7.

here, or in thy lifetime they all perish, and thou failest in thy trust."[117]

It is therefore not despising the needs and helps of earthly friends and of our fellow creatures to say that we should not put entire trust in them for all the wants and demands of our being. They are good, they were made by God, they are oftentimes able to assist us — nay, we need them to a certain extent — but, because of the extent of our wants, they are utterly unable to satisfy us completely, even if they desired to do so.

And even if creatures could give us a partial contentment, as at times they seem to do, we know that it cannot last, and in the midst of our joy and pleasure, we are haunted by the thought that someday, too soon, it all must pass away. We are seeking for rest, for peace, for happiness — all unending; we want something to steady our lives and satisfy the yearnings of our souls forever. But we must not look for these things in the world, for the world at best is passing away.[118] There is no stability to human things; the cloud and the storm swiftly follow

---

[117]St. Augustine, Exposition 2 on Psalm 30 (RSV = Ps. 31).
[118]Cf. 1 Cor. 7:31.

the sunshine; we have no lasting habitation here below.[119] Today we are sitting at the banquet of pleasure; tomorrow we are draining the cup of sorrow. Today we receive the applause of men; tomorrow we may be the objects of their scorn. Today we put forth the tender leaves of hope; tomorrow there comes a killing frost that ruins all our prospects.

∞

God alone can satisfy you

Such, then, is the lot of man when considered in his relations to creatures and to the world. Man's lot is full of uncertainty, instability, and vicissitude. But this should not make us skeptical or cynical; it affords no justification for pessimism. It is a condition arising, on the one hand, from the very nature of limited beings, and on the other, from the vast potentialities of our souls, which, while they are limited in giving to others, cannot be appeased except by the God who made them.

There is a craving in the heart of man for something which the world cannot give. He clutches for the things that are passing, he toils, he labors, he struggles; he

[119]Cf. Heb. 13:14.

strives for money, for power, for place, for honor — not because any of these things are in themselves what he desires, but only because he conceives them as means and helps to the satisfaction, to the stillness of mind, peace of heart, and rest of soul and body for which his nature longs. Peace and happiness and contentment of life are the objects of all our dreams, of our persistent efforts, of our ambitions and aims; but until we give up the hope of finding these things in the world, in our fellow mortals, in anything short of God, we shall never know the blessedness for which we yearn. If we would ever attain to the state which we covet, we must learn the lesson, even though it be through tears and sorrow, that God alone, who made our souls with all their vast desires, is able to comfort us and steady our lives amid the storms and distresses of earth.

It is futile to trust in men, or "in the children of men, in whom there is no salvation."[120] The peace and blessedness which we seek are "not as the world giveth."[121] and unless we turn away from the world and cease to torture

[120]Ps. 145:3 (RSV = Ps. 146:3).
[121]John 14:27.

179

our lives with its vanities, our portion can never be other than heartaches, secret loathing, and consuming thirst. "For many friends cannot profit," says Thomas à Kempis, "nor strong helpers assist, nor prudent counselors give a profitable answer, nor the books of the learned afford comfort, nor any precious substance deliver, nor any place, however retired and lovely, give shelter, unless Thou Thyself dost assist, help, strengthen, console, instruct, and guard us."[122] Such has been the history of the race, and such is the experience of every individual in the race who has placed his hope and trust in anything created.

We are confronted, therefore, on the one side, by the inherent weakness of our own nature and the constant needs that arise therefrom; and, on the other side, we are assured by the history of the race, if not by our own experience, that so long as we strive to satisfy our wants by an appeal to anything but God, we are doomed to disappointment and sorrow.

It is unfortunate that most people must first be crushed by the world and creatures which they serve

---

[122] *Imitation of Christ*, Bk. 3, ch. 59.

before they grasp the fundamental truth that creatures are not their God. Comparatively few of those who enjoy the world are ever brought to realize the dignity and divine purpose of their souls until the world and its allurements, like a false pageant on a false stage, give way beneath them, and they fall helpless and alone. It is commonly only after repeated awful experiences, when worn out and exhausted by years of fruitless quests for peace and happiness and contentment, that men wake up to the simple fact that the treasures which they seek are not in the world, nor as the world gives.

You must turn to God

But it is one thing to turn away from the world disappointed, disgusted, and betrayed; and it is quite another thing to turn to God and to recognize Him as our good Father and Shepherd, patiently waiting to receive us, ever able and ready to satisfy our wants. There are many people who find the world a disappointment and a deception, and who turn from it with loathing and hatred, but fail ever to lift their weary eyes to the proper object of their trust. Like the Israelites of old, they succeed at length in escaping from the hands of oppression and

tyranny, but only to wander in a desert land throughout
the length of their days. This is the region where dwell
the pessimist, the skeptic, and the cynic — miserable
mortals who have wasted on creatures the talents they
should have given to their Creator, or who have otherwise failed in their conception of life, and have left
unmultiplied the money of the Master.[123]

There is plainly no middle course for us if we do not
wish to encounter disaster. It is not enough for us to turn
from positive harm, from the objects that deceive and
disappoint us; we must further turn to positive good, and
to Him who alone can quiet and appease our yearning
spirits.

One of the most evident and convincing reasons, then,
why we should put our trust in God above all else is that
He alone can satisfy us and give us rest. Only God is able
adequately to respond to all the needs of our being. The
simplest process of reasoning should assure us of this,
when once we perceive the vastness of our wants and the
impossibility of their satisfaction through the medium
of created things. We know that our nature, which has

[123]Cf. Matt. 25:24-30.

come from the source and essence of truth, cannot be false. Neither can our unlimited capacities for knowledge, for joy, and for happiness be a deceiving mockery.

There is a way to peace for us, and a source of supreme contentment; there is a fountain of living waters from which, if we drink, we shall never thirst again. Hence our Savior said, "Come to me, all you that labor and are burdened, and I will refresh you";[124] and again, "He that shall drink of the water that I will give him shall not thirst forever; but the water that I will give him shall become in him a fountain of water, springing up into life everlasting."[125]

But we shall never be able to come to God, we shall never succeed even in getting near the secret of interior peace and contentment until we are able to grasp more or less comprehensively the great basic truths of our existence: that God loves each one of us with the love of an infinite Father, and that His Providence is so universal and omnipotent as to extend to all things, even to the numbering of the hairs of our head.[126] We talk much

[124]Matt. 11:28.
[125]John 4:13-14.
[126]Matt. 10:30; Luke 12:7.

about chance and fortune and accident. We speak every day of things happening, as if by the sheerest contingence, without warning or previous knowledge. And so it is with reference to ourselves, and to all the world, perhaps. But with reference to Divine Providence, it is not so; there is nothing accidental, nothing unforeseen, with respect to God. "Without Thy counsel and Providence, and without cause, nothing cometh to pass in the earth,"[127] says the *Imitation*.

But what does this mean: "God provides"? It means that the will of the omnipotent Father directs and governs everything. "Providence," says St. John Damascene, "is the will of God, by which all things are fitly and harmoniously governed,"[128] and such is its power that nothing can elude or deceive it, neither can it be hindered or baffled in any way. "For God will not except any man's person; neither will He stand in awe of any man's greatness; for He made the little and the great, and He hath equally care of all."[129]

[127] *Imitation of Christ*, Bk. 3, ch. 50.
[128] St. John Damascene (c. 675-c. 749; Greek theologian and Doctor), *De Fide Orthodoxa*, Bk. 2, sect. 29.
[129] Wisd. 6:8.

∞

God controls all of life's events

And just as Divine Providence disposes and governs all the events of life, directing each to its proper end, so the divine will is the cause of everything that exists. Just as it is impossible that anything should escape God's knowledge and directing hand, so is it impossible that anything should exist or come into being without the direct intervention or permission of His will. There is nothing in the world which God has not made, and nothing takes place which is not according to His good pleasure, except the malice and guilt of sin. All the other evils of life, such as sickness, suffering, disease, poverty, cold, hunger, thirst, and the like, God actually wills. And precisely because these things proceed from His will, they cannot be bad.

God is the author of all good, and He cannot do evil. So good, indeed, is He that, if He were not sufficiently omnipotent to draw good out of evil, He would never have permitted any evil to exist. "God has judged it better," says St. Augustine, "to work good out of evil, than to allow no evil."[130]

---

[130]St. Augustine, *Enchiridion*, Bk. 3, no. 27.

We must not argue in our foolishness and try to understand all the doings of God, for His ways are not our ways; His thoughts not our thoughts.[131] It is often beyond our power even to understand our fellow creatures, so how foolish it is to complain because we cannot comprehend the great Creator! It is enough for us, if we are sincere and right of heart, to know, as we do, that God is good, that He loves us individually, and that His protecting hand guides and governs all the events of our lives, even to the smallest detail. These are truths which we must take hold of and lay close to our hearts, or else we shall go the way of error and issue in ultimate disaster.

And from these truths, so certain and unquestionable, it further follows that everything existing in the world, so far as it affects us, everything that falls to our lot, all that we encounter, all that we suffer, all that we do, aside from sin, has been purposely arranged by Almighty God for our greater spiritual good and eternal salvation. This must be so, since God is the universal cause of all things, and since He sincerely loves us and desires above all to

[131]Isa. 55:8; Rom. 11:33.

save us. If it were otherwise, either He would not have omnipotent control of everything, or He could not be said really to desire our salvation.

How sadly we misunderstand these great truths in our daily lives, when we murmur and complain at the evils that afflict us! How narrowly we conceive the all-powerful will of God, and the infinite abyss of His goodness which would lead us to eternal delights!

We would like to escape all the evils of time; we love our lives, and we wish to save them from final wreck; but, failing to trust in the will of God, we forget the words of Christ: "He that loveth his life shall lose it; and he that hateth his life in this world, keepeth it unto life eternal."[132] We want to save our souls, and we are, perhaps, much disturbed about doing many and great things in the cause of God and of Heaven, while unmindful of the Master's warning that, "not everyone that saith to me, 'Lord, Lord,' shall enter into the kingdom of Heaven; but he that doth the will of my Father who is in Heaven, he shall enter into the kingdom of Heaven."[133] It is doubtless

[132]John 12:25.
[133]Matt. 7:21.

our aim to draw ever nearer and nearer to our Savior, and to deepen our relationship with Him; but do we remember that He said, "Whosoever shall do the will of God, he is my brother, and my sister, and mother"?[134]

"Yes," you will say, "This is all true. I know it is so; my faith is at fault. If I only had that beautiful faith and trust in God which many have, it would be easy for me, and I would be happy! Faith is a gift, and favored are they who possess it."

∞

Pray for the wisdom of the Cross

But, dear reader, can you not pray? Can you not ask from God that heavenly gift which will move mountains and transplant them into the sea?[135] Can you not overcome your indolence and your repugnance, and patiently and persistently implore from on high that superior vision which pierces the clouds and sees in everything the hand of God? Surely you can say, with the devout author of the *Imitation of Christ*, "Behold, O beloved Father, I am in Thy hands; I bow myself under the rod of Thy

---

[134]Mark 3:35.
[135]Cf. Mark 11:23.

correction. Strike my back and my neck, too, that my crookedness may be conformed to Thy will."[136] Here again, you should remember the words of your Savior: "The kingdom of Heaven suffereth violence, and the violent bear it away."[137]

Perhaps the greatest trial to our faith in Divine Providence is in bearing what we call the wrongs of life. That we should have any crosses to suffer at all; that there should be death and sickness and disease; that there should be poverty and misery, distress and worry, labor and sorrow; that there should exist any of these things is to our infirmity if we forget our sins and the sins of our race that have caused these evils, which are a trial and a test of fidelity.

But it is still more difficult, except to minds that are deeply religious, to meet, with the gentleness and serenity of faith, the positive injuries — the injustice, the scorn, the ridicule, the pain and persecution which others, needy creatures like ourselves, actually inflict upon us. It is easier, we say, to bear poverty than insult; it is

[136]*Imitation of Christ*, Bk. 3, ch. 50.
[137]Matt. 11:12.

easier to suffer the inclemency of the elements than to endure the unkindness of our brethren; it is easier to put up with the pain and weariness of bodily sickness than to come under the lash of the tongues of men.

There is here, however, no room for hesitation and question; the rule is the same for all the crosses that come to us. God often permits us to be afflicted by the sins of others for our greater spiritual profit. Since, therefore, all alike proceed from God, either by positive act or divine permission, and since we know that He is supremely good and loves us, having given every proof of His desire to save us, even to the delivering up of His only Son,[138] we can never reasonably or sincerely doubt that every evil and cross of life, with the sole exception of our personal sins, has been arranged for our good.

My God, teach us the wisdom of the Cross!

"For this is a favor to Thy friend, that for love of Thee, he may suffer and be afflicted in the world, howsoever often and by whomsoever Thou permittest such trials to befall him."[139]

---

[138] Rom. 8:32.

[139] *Imitation of Christ*, Bk. 3, ch. 50.

∞

See God's loving hand even in your sufferings
It is helpful that here also, in learning to discern
the source and meaning of our afflictions, we have ever
before us the examples of the holiest souls. We know
that in all trials, they steadfastly look beyond the cross
that presses them, to the hand of Him who has placed
it there. Like the shepherd's sheep, they are convinced
of the power and goodness of their Master, and nothing
can shake their trust in Him. Without distinction or
question, they accept all as coming from God by special
act or sovereign permission, to purify them, to detach
them from the world and creatures, to increase their
nearness and likeness to Himself, to multiply their
merits for Heaven and bring them to everlasting crowns.

They discover the workings of Providence every-
where, in things that are painful, as well as in things that
are pleasant to nature. Thus, behind their pangs of body
and mind, behind the whips and scorns of time, behind
the tongue that slanders and calumniates them, behind
the oppressor's wrong, the injustice and tyranny of princes
and rulers, behind all the evils of life, they see the hand
of Him who directs and governs all.

But here we must not conclude that the saints and holy persons have never resisted evil and evildoers, and that consequently we must not. This would be a serious mistake, as Church history and hagiography plainly prove. Who was ever more vigorous and fearless in opposing wrong and the doers of wrong than St. Paul, St. Augustine, and St. Jerome?[140] Who was ever more persistent in his efforts to prevail against the evils of sin in others than St. Monica, St. Teresa, St. Dominic, and St. Catherine of Siena?[141]

After their example, then, we may, and we must, struggle against evils of all kinds, whether physical or spiritual, whether from ourselves or from others, insofar as it is not certain that it is the will of God that we should submit to them.

But when we have exerted ourselves reasonably and lawfully to rid our lives of that which afflicts us, and still it persists, there can be no further doubt that it is the will

[140]St. Jerome (c. 342-420), biblical scholar.

[141]St. Monica (c. 331-387), mother of St. Augustine; St. Teresa (1515-1582), Spanish Carmelite nun and mystic; St. Dominic (1170-1221), founder of the Order of Friars Preachers; St. Catherine of Siena (c. 1347-1380), Dominican tertiary.

of God that we should patiently and submissively accept our condition and our cross. Since, however, we do not know how long it is the wish of Providence that we should be burdened and afflicted, we may continue patiently to use every legitimate means to be delivered, provided it be done with humble resignation to the will of our heavenly Father.

The acceptance of injuries, therefore, on the part of holy souls is not a weak yielding to inevitable circumstances, nor a willing consent to the wrongs of others. Like St. Paul, they know whom they have believed,[142] and they are certain that, in due time, divine justice will bring all evildoers to an evil end and will deliver the just from their troubles.

And further, when the vengeance of the persecutor is turned upon them, and they are hunted down without reason by their kind — even by the members of their own household — they remember the words of their Shepherd: "The disciple is not above his master, nor the servant above his lord. It is enough for the disciple that he be as his master, and the servant as his lord. If they

---

[142]Cf. 2 Tim. 1:12.

have called the good man of the house Beelzebub, how much more them of his household?"[143]

And again, when the servants of God behold the wicked prospering and the just oppressed, when they see the ambitious, the covetous, and the unscrupulous preferred and honored, and they themselves plotted against and rejected, their hearts are not disturbed, because they know, first of all, that "to them that love God, all things work together unto good,"[144] and second, they are persuaded that the efforts of sinners must finally fail. "For the hope of the wicked is as dust, which is blown away with the wind, and as a thin froth which is dispersed by the storm, and as a smoke that is scattered abroad by the wind, and as the remembrance of a guest of one day that passeth by."[145]

In a word, then, those who are really the friends of God have faith and confidence in their heavenly Master; and all the perils of earth, and all the powers of darkness cannot avail to daunt them or turn them aside from their purpose.

[143]Matt. 10:24-25.
[144]Rom. 8:28.
[145]Wisd. 5:15.

It is this steadfastness of religious trust that we, too, must strive to acquire. It is the only way to peace and victory. If we wish ever to rise above the evils of our lives, we must learn to look to God for everything. And we must look to God not only as to a bountiful benefactor, but as to a kind master who knows how best to discipline his servants and preserve them from irreparable harm.

God arranges everything for your good

There is a substantially correct translation of the final verse of the shepherd psalm, which may be rendered as follows: "And Thy goodness and kindness pursue me all the days of my life, that I may dwell in the house of the Lord forever." It is the special wording of the second clause of the stanza that expresses the real purpose of Divine Providence in regard to the elect. Everything in life has been ordained and arranged for their eternal salvation, and for the increase of their heavenly rewards.

"Therefore," wrote St. Paul, "I endure all things for the sake of the elect, that they also may obtain the salvation, which is in Christ Jesus, with heavenly glory."[146] It

---

[146] 2 Tim. 2:10.

is this firm conviction that infinite love is at the bottom of all the workings of Providence, doing everything for the sake of the elect, that consoles and steadies the souls of the just throughout all the trials and crosses of life. In the thick of the battle, they never lose sight of the faithful Shepherd who leads them, and they ever behold by faith the unspeakable delights He has prepared for them who love Him.[147]

What joys are there in our faith and hope! If, by the mercy and goodness of God, we succeed in saving our souls, how cheap will seem the price we shall have paid for Heaven, and how benign and ineffably loving will appear the Providence of God, which is leading us there!

At times now, in our fervor, we can faintly and feebly imagine what it will mean to throw off forever this veil of faith and see distinctly and continually the Shepherd of our souls. But our liveliest conceptions here are infinitely inferior to the vision to come. It is only when the veil shall have been removed that we shall fully realize how the goodness and mercy of God have always pursued

[147]Cf. 1 Cor. 2:9.

us in this life, that we might be saved and enjoy the rewards of His house forever.

May God give us all that childlike trust in our heavenly Master which the sheep display toward their shepherd. May He grant us that vivid constant faith of the saints, which will enable us to see in every event of life — in adversity as well as in prosperity, in our pains as well as in our joys — the designs of a loving Father who is ever wishing and trying to lead His children to His home of eternal delights.

Biographical Note

Charles J. Callan, O.P.

(1877-1962)

Born in Royalton, New York, in 1877, the young Charles Callan aspired to a career as a lawyer and orator. "There was glory, fame, distinction, wealth, applause, all gleaming and waiting, as it were, in the golden sunshine of the morning of life, and beckoning to me."[148] But a moving sermon by a young Dominican priest transformed him, and holiness, rather than worldly glory, became his ambition.

With his sights now set on becoming a sacred orator and writer, Callan studied at the Jesuit-run Canisius

---

[148]Walter Romig, *The Book of Catholic Authors*, 2nd ser. (Grosse Pointe, Michigan: Walter Romig and Company, 1943), 53.

College in Buffalo, New York, with the intention of entering the Society of Jesus. But realizing that Jesuit life would be too rigorous for his frail health, which had troubled him since childhood, he entered the Dominican novitiate at Springfield, Kentucky, where he met another novice, John McHugh, who was to be his close friend for life.

After his Ordination to the priesthood, Fr. Callan taught philosophy for six years at the Dominican House of Studies in Washington, DC, but because of his poor health, he was assigned, along with Fr. McHugh, to a parish in Hawthorne, New York, and to a teaching position at nearby Maryknoll Seminary.

In 1916, Fr. Callan and Fr. McHugh became editors of *Homiletic and Pastoral Review,* which grew in influence under their editorship, and participated in the founding of two Dominican quarterlies: *Dominicana* and *The Thomist.* The two priests collaborated on the writing and editing of dozens of works, including books, devotional volumes, a translation of the New Testament from the original Greek, and, with Fr. Callan's brother Frank, a book on English prose style. A preaching program developed by the two Dominicans at the request of

Archbishop Hayes became the official program for the Archdiocese of New York for twelve years.

Fr. Callan himself was an editor of the Confraternity edition of the New Testament, as well as the author of numerous articles on Scripture, dogma, moral theology, devotion, and the Liturgy. In 1940, he was honored by Pope Pius XII, who appointed him Consultor to the Pontifical Biblical Commission. His other achievements and honors include the degree of Lector of Sacred Theology from the University of Fribourg, Switzerland, in 1908; an honorary degree of Doctor of Literature from Gonzaga College, Washington, DC, in 1925; and a Master of Sacred Theology degree from the Angelicum in Rome in 1931.

Fr. Callan's passion for writing went beyond a love for language to an understanding and communication of truths. "The would-be writer," he said, "must go from his books to life, must ponder the difference between theory and practice, must compare the ideal and the real. Only then will he be speaking *to* men instead of *about* them, and in terms which mean anything to them."[149] This

[149]Ibid., 58-59.

Your Soul's Gentle Shepherd

philosophy of learning and writing is reflected in his works, which delve into the richness of Scripture and reveal how sacred truths affect the life of every individual. Fr. Callan's consoling wisdom awakens today's Christians to hear God's message and to see more clearly His loving presence in their lives.

Sophia Institute Press®

Sophia Institute is a nonprofit institution that seeks to restore man's knowledge of eternal truth, including man's knowledge of his own nature, his relation to other persons, and his relation to God.

Sophia Institute Press® serves this end in numerous ways. It publishes translations of foreign works to make them accessible for the first time to English-speaking readers. It brings back into print books that have long been out of print. And it publishes important new books that fulfill the ideals of Sophia Institute. These books afford readers a rich source of the enduring wisdom of mankind. Sophia Institute Press® makes these high-quality books available to the general public by using advanced technology and by soliciting donations to subsidize its general publishing costs. Your generosity can help Sophia Institute Press® to provide the public with editions of works containing the enduring wisdom of the ages. Please send your tax-deductible contribution to the address below. We also welcome your questions, comments, and suggestions.

For your free catalog, call:
Toll-free: 1-800-888-9344

or write:
Sophia Institute Press®
Box 5284, Manchester, NH 03108

or visit our website:
www.sophiainstitute.com